# FUNDAMENTALS OF

# ENGLISH GRAMMAR

Third Edition

# CHARTBOOK

## A Reference Grammar

## Betty Schrampfer Azar

Longman

**Fundamentals of English Grammar, Third Edition**
**Chartbook**

Azar Associates
Shelley Hartle, Editor
Susan Van Etten, Manager

Pearson Education, 10 Bank Street, White Plains, NY 10606

Vice president of instructional design: Allen Ascher
Editorial manager: Pam Fishman
Project manager: Margo Grant
Development editor: Janet Johnston
Vice president, director of design and production: Rhea Banker
Director of electronic production: Aliza Greenblatt
Executive managing editor: Linda Moser
Production manager: Ray Keating
Production editor: Robert Ruvo
Director of manufacturing: Patrice Fraccio
Senior manufacturing buyer: Edie Pullman
Cover design: Monika Popowitz
Text composition: Carlisle Communications, Ltd.
Text font: 9.5/10 Plantin

ISBN: 0-13-013635-2

Printed in the United States of America
7 8 9 10 11 12 –V011– 15 14 13 12 11

# Contents

# Preface

This *Chartbook* contains examples and explanations of English grammar for intermediate students of English as a second or foreign language. It is intended principally as an accompaniment to the *Workbook* for *Fundamentals of English Grammar.*

The practices in the *Workbook* are cross-referenced to the charts in this book. This handbook–workbook combination is especially suited to teaching situations where the students need to do much practicing and studying on their own outside the classroom. The *Workbook* contains a wealth of self-study practices, with a removable answer key provided at the back of the book. The *Chartbook* serves as a reference text.

The *Teacher's Guide* for *Fundamentals of English Grammar* contains additional notes on many grammar points; each chart is discussed and amplified.

# CHAPTER 1
# Present Time

## CONTENTS

## 1-1  THE SIMPLE PRESENT AND THE PRESENT PROGRESSIVE

| THE SIMPLE PRESENT 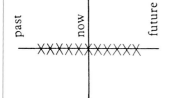 | (a) Ann **takes** a shower *every day*.<br>(b) I *usually* **read** the newspaper in the morning.<br>(c) Babies **cry**.  Birds **fly**.<br><br>(d) NEGATIVE:<br>It **doesn't snow** in Bangkok.<br>(e) QUESTION:<br>**Does** the teacher **speak** slowly? | The SIMPLE PRESENT expresses *daily habits* or *usual activities*, as in (a) and (b).<br>The simple present expresses *general statements of fact*, as in (c).<br>In sum, the simple present is used for events or situations that exist always, usually, or habitually in the past, present, and future. |
|---|---|---|
| THE PRESENT PROGRESSIVE 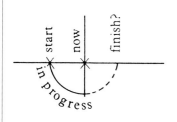 | (f) Ann can't come to the phone *right now* because she **is taking** a shower.<br>(g) I **am reading** my grammar book *right now*.<br>(h) Jimmy and Susie are babies.  They **are crying**.  I can hear them *right now*.  Maybe they are hungry.<br>(i) NEGATIVE:<br>It **isn't snowing** *right now*.<br>(j) QUESTION:<br>**Is** the teacher **speaking** *right now*? | The PRESENT PROGRESSIVE expresses *an activity that is in progress (is occurring, is happening) right now*.  The event is in progress at the time the speaker is saying the sentence.  The event began in the past, is in progress now, and will probably continue into the future.<br>FORM: ***am, is, are* + *-ing***. |

**FORMS OF THE SIMPLE PRESENT AND THE PRESENT PROGRESSIVE**

|  | SIMPLE PRESENT | PRESENT PROGRESSIVE |
|---|---|---|
| STATEMENT | I-You-We-They **work**.<br>He-She-It **works**. | I **am** **working**.<br>You-We-They **are** **working**.<br>He-She-It **is** **working**. |
| NEGATIVE | I-You-We-They **do** **not** **work**.<br>He-She-It **does** **not** **work**. | I **am** **not** **working**.<br>You-We-They **are** **not** **working**.<br>He-She-It **is** **not** **working**. |
| QUESTION | **Do** I-you-we-they **work?**<br>**Does** he-she-it **work?** | **Am** I **working?**<br>**Are** you-we-they **working?**<br>**Is** he-she-it **working?** |
| CONTRACTIONS<br><br>pronoun + *be* | *I* + *am* = **I'm** working.<br>*you, we, they* + *are* = **You're, We're, They're** working.<br>*he, she, it* + *is* = **He's, She's, It's** working. | |
| *do + not* | *does* + *not* = **doesn't**    She **doesn't** work.<br>*do* + *not* = **don't**    I **don't** work. | |
| *be + not* | *is* + *not* = **isn't**    He **isn't** working.<br>*are* + *not* = **aren't**    They **aren't** working.<br>*(am* + *not* = am not★    I am not working.) | |

★Note: *am* and *not* are not contracted.

It's 7:30 A.M., and the Wilsons are in their kitchen.
Mrs. Wilson *is sitting* at the breakfast table.  She *'s reading* a newspaper.
She *reads* the newspaper every morning.

## 1-3 FREQUENCY ADVERBS

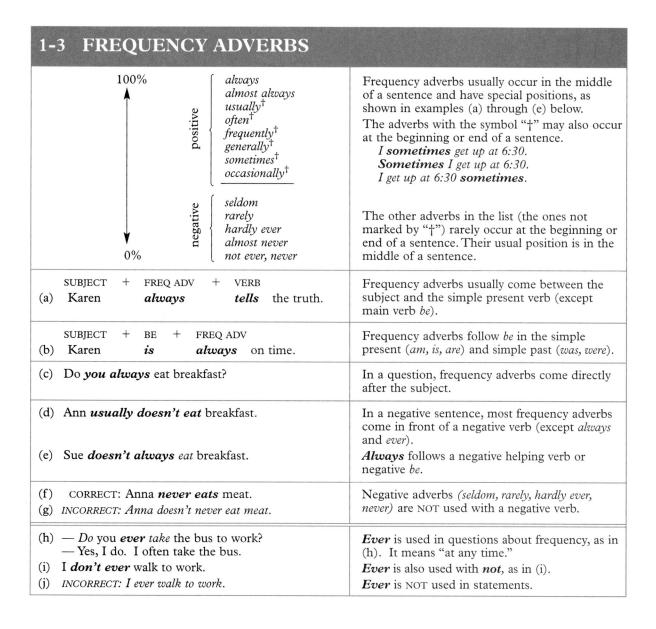

| | |
|---|---|
| 100% ↑ positive: *always* / *almost always* / *usually*† / *often*† / *frequently*† / *generally*† / *sometimes*† / *occasionally*† <br><br> negative: *seldom* / *rarely* / *hardly ever* / *almost never* / *not ever, never* <br> 0% ↓ | Frequency adverbs usually occur in the middle of a sentence and have special positions, as shown in examples (a) through (e) below. <br> The adverbs with the symbol "†" may also occur at the beginning or end of a sentence. <br>   *I **sometimes** get up at 6:30.* <br>   ***Sometimes** I get up at 6:30.* <br>   *I get up at 6:30 **sometimes**.* <br><br> The other adverbs in the list (the ones not marked by "†") rarely occur at the beginning or end of a sentence. Their usual position is in the middle of a sentence. |
| (a)   SUBJECT  +  FREQ ADV  +  VERB <br>      Karen       ***always***      ***tells***  the truth. | Frequency adverbs usually come between the subject and the simple present verb (except main verb *be*). |
| (b)   SUBJECT  +  BE  +  FREQ ADV <br>      Karen      ***is***    ***always***  on time. | Frequency adverbs follow *be* in the simple present (*am, is, are*) and simple past (*was, were*). |
| (c)   Do ***you always*** eat breakfast? | In a question, frequency adverbs come directly after the subject. |
| (d)   Ann ***usually doesn't eat*** breakfast. <br><br> (e)   Sue ***doesn't always*** eat breakfast. | In a negative sentence, most frequency adverbs come in front of a negative verb (except *always* and *ever*). <br> ***Always*** follows a negative helping verb or negative *be*. |
| (f)   CORRECT: Anna ***never eats*** meat. <br> (g)   INCORRECT: *Anna doesn't never eat meat.* | Negative adverbs *(seldom, rarely, hardly ever, never)* are NOT used with a negative verb. |
| (h)   — *Do* you ***ever** take* the bus to work? <br>      — Yes, I do. I often take the bus. <br> (i)   I ***don't ever*** walk to work. <br> (j)   INCORRECT: *I ever walk to work.* | ***Ever*** is used in questions about frequency, as in (h). It means "at any time." <br> ***Ever*** is also used with ***not***, as in (i). <br> ***Ever*** is NOT used in statements. |

## 1-4 FINAL -S

| | |
|---|---|
| (a) SINGULAR: *one bird* <br> (b) PLURAL: *two birds, three birds, many birds, all birds, etc.* | SINGULAR = one, not two or more <br> PLURAL = two, three, or more |
| (c) **Bird**s sing. <br> (d) A bird **sings**. | **A plural noun** ends in **-s**, as in (c). <br> **A singular verb** ends in **-s**, as in (d). |
| (e) **A bird** *sings* outside my window. <br>      **It** *sings* loudly. <br>   **Ann** *sings* beautifully. <br>   **She** *sings* songs to her children. <br>   **Tom** *sings* very well. <br>     **He** *sings* in a chorus. | A singular verb follows a singular subject. <br> Add **-s** to the simple present verb if the subject is <br>   (1) a singular noun (e.g., *a bird, Ann, Tom*) or <br>   (2) *he, she,* or *it*.★ |

★*He, she,* and *it* are third person singular personal pronouns. See Chart 6-10, p. 44, for more information about personal pronouns.

## 1-5 SPELLING OF FINAL -S/-ES

| | |
|---|---|
| (a) visit → ***visits*** <br>   speak → ***speaks*** <br> (b) ride → ***rides*** <br>   write → ***writes*** | Final **-s**, not **-es**, is added to most verbs. <br> (INCORRECT: *visites, speakes*) <br> Many verbs end in **-e**. Final **-s** is simply added. |
| (c) catch → ***catches*** <br>   wash → ***washes*** <br>   miss → ***misses*** <br>   fix → ***fixes*** <br>   buzz → ***buzzes*** | Final **-es** is added to words that end in **-ch, -sh, -s, -x,** and **-z**. <br> PRONUNCIATION NOTE: Final **-es** is pronounced /əz/ and adds a syllable.★ |
| (d) **fly** → ***flies*** | If a word ends in a consonant + **-y**, change the **-y** to **-i** and add **-es**. <br> (INCORRECT: *flys*) |
| (e) pay → ***pays*** | If a word ends in a vowel + **-y**, simply add **-s**.★★ <br> (INCORRECT: *paies* or *payes*) |
| (f) go → ***goes*** /gowz/ <br>   do → ***does*** /dəz/ <br>   have → ***has*** /hæz/ | The singular forms of the verbs *go, do,* and *have* are irregular. |

★See Chart 6-1, p. 38, for more information about the pronunciation of final **-s/-es**.
★★Vowels = a, e, i, o, u. Consonants = all other letters in the alphabet.

## 1-6 NON-ACTION VERBS

| | |
|---|---|
| (a) I **know** Ms. Chen.<br>  INCORRECT: *I am knowing Ms. Chen.*<br>(b) I'm hungry. I **want** a sandwich.<br>  INCORRECT: *I am wanting a sandwich.*<br>(c) This book **belongs** to Mikhail.<br>  INCORRECT: *This book is belonging to Mikhail.* | Some verbs are not used in progressive tenses. These verbs are called "non-action verbs." They express a situation that exists, not an action in progress. |

NON-ACTION VERBS★

| | | | | | | |
|---|---|---|---|---|---|---|
| hear | believe | be | own | need | like | forget |
| see | think† | exist | have† | want | love | remember |
| sound | understand | | possess | prefer | hate | |
| | know | | belong | | | |

| | |
|---|---|
| †COMPARE<br><br>(d) I **think** that grammar is easy.<br><br>(e) I **am thinking** about grammar right now.<br><br>(f) Tom **has** a car.<br><br>(g) I**'m having** a good time. | *Think* and *have* can be used in the progressive.<br>In (d): When **think** means "believe," it is nonprogressive.<br>In (e): When **think** expresses thoughts that are going through a person's mind, it can be progressive.<br>In (f): When **have** means "own" or expresses possession, it is not used in the progressive.<br>In (g): In expressions where **have** does not mean "own" (e.g., *have a good time, have a bad time, have trouble, have a problem, have company, have an operation*), **have** can be used in the progressive. |

*Non-action verbs are also called "stative verbs" or "nonprogressive verbs."

## 1-7 PRESENT VERBS: SHORT ANSWERS TO YES/NO QUESTIONS

| | QUESTION | SHORT ANSWER | LONG ANSWER |
|---|---|---|---|
| QUESTIONS WITH *DO/DOES* | *Does* Bob *like* tea? | Yes, he **does**.<br>No, he **doesn't**. | Yes, he likes tea.<br>No, he doesn't like tea. |
| | *Do* you *like* tea? | Yes, I **do**.<br>No, I **don't**. | Yes, I like tea.<br>No, I don't like tea. |
| QUESTIONS WITH *BE* | *Are* you *studying?* | Yes, I **am**.★<br>No, I**'m not**. | Yes, I am (I'm) studying.<br>No, I'm not studying. |
| | *Is* Yoko a student? | Yes, she **is**.★<br>No, she**'s not**. OR<br>No, she **isn't**. | Yes, she is (she's) a student.<br>No, she's not a student. OR<br>No, she isn't a student. |
| | *Are* they *studying?* | Yes, they **are**.★<br>No, they**'re not**. OR<br>No, they **aren't**. | Yes, they are (they're) studying.<br>No, they're not studying. OR<br>No, they aren't studying. |

★*Am, is,* and *are* are not contracted with pronouns in short answers.
  INCORRECT SHORT ANSWERS: *Yes, I'm. Yes, she's. Yes, they're.*

# CHAPTER 2
## Past Time

### CONTENTS

## 2-1  EXPRESSING PAST TIME: THE SIMPLE PAST

| | |
|---|---|
| (a) Mary **walked** downtown *yesterday*. <br> (b) I **slept** for eight hours *last night*. | The simple past is used to talk about activities or situations that began and ended in the past (e.g., *yesterday, last night, two days ago, in 1999*). |
| (c) Bob **stayed** home yesterday morning. <br> (d) Our plane **arrived** on time last night. | Most simple past verbs are formed by adding **-ed** to a verb, as in (a), (c), and (d). |
| (e) I **ate** breakfast this morning. <br> (f) Sue **took** a taxi to the airport yesterday. | Some verbs have irregular past forms, as in (b), (e), and (f). See Chart 2-7, p. 10. |
| (g) I **was** busy yesterday. <br> (h) They **were** at home last night. | The simple past forms of **be** are **was** and **were**. |

The bear **slept** in a cave last winter.

## 2-2 FORMS OF THE SIMPLE PAST: REGULAR VERBS

| STATEMENT | I-You-She-He-It-We-They *worked* yesterday. |
|---|---|
| NEGATIVE | I-You-She-He-It-We-They *did not (didn't) work* yesterday. |
| QUESTION | *Did* I-you-she-he-it-we-they *work* yesterday? |
| SHORT ANSWER | Yes, I-you-she-he-it-we-they *did*.<br>No, I-you-she-he-it-we-they *didn't*. |

## 2-3 FORMS OF THE SIMPLE PAST: *BE*

| STATEMENT | I-She-He-It *was* in class yesterday.<br>We-You-They *were* in class yesterday. |
|---|---|
| NEGATIVE | I-She-He-It *was not (wasn't)* in class yesterday.<br>We-You-They *were not (weren't)* in class yesterday. |
| QUESTION | *Was* I-she-he-it in class yesterday?<br>*Were* we-you-they in class yesterday? |
| SHORT ANSWER | Yes, I-she-he-it *was*.     Yes, we-you-they *were*.<br>No, I-she-he-it *wasn't*.     No, we-you-they *weren't*. |

## 2-4 REGULAR VERBS: PRONUNCIATION OF *-ED* ENDINGS

| | |
|---|---|
| (a) talked   = talk/t/<br>     stopped  = stop/t/<br>     hissed   = hiss/t/<br>     watched = watch/t/<br>     washed  = wash/t/ | Final *-ed* is pronounced /t/ after voiceless sounds.<br>You make a voiceless sound by pushing air through your mouth. No sound comes from your throat.<br>Examples of voiceless sounds: /k/, /p/, /s/, /ch/, /sh/. |
| (b) called   = call/d/<br>     rained  = rain/d/<br>     lived   = live/d/<br>     robbed  = rob/d/<br>     stayed  = stay/d/ | Final *-ed* is pronounced /d/ after voiced sounds.<br>You make a voiced sound from your throat. Your voice box vibrates.<br>Examples of voiced sounds: /l/, /n/, /v/, /b/, and all vowel sounds. |
| (c) waited   = wait/əd/<br>     needed  = need/əd/ | Final *-ed* is pronounced /əd/ after "t" and "d" sounds. /əd/ adds a syllable to a word. |

## 2-5 SPELLING OF -ING AND -ED FORMS

| END OF VERB | DOUBLE THE CONSONANT? | SIMPLE FORM | -ING | -ED | |
|---|---|---|---|---|---|
| *-e* | NO | (a) smil**e**<br>hop**e** | smiling<br>hoping | smiled<br>hoped | **-ing** form: Drop the **-e**, add **-ing**.<br>**-ed** form: Just add **-d**. |
| Two Consonants | NO | (b) he**lp**<br>lea**rn** | helping<br>learning | helped<br>learned | If the verb ends in two consonants, just add **-ing** or **-ed**. |
| Two Vowels + One Consonant | NO | (c) **rain**<br>**heat** | raining<br>heating | rained<br>heated | If the verb ends in two vowels + a consonant, just add **-ing** or **-ed**. |
| One Vowel + One Consonant | YES | ONE-SYLLABLE VERBS<br>(d) sto**p**<br>pla**n** | stopping<br>planning | stopped<br>planned | If the verb has one syllable and ends in one vowel + one consonant, double the consonant to make the **-ing** or **-ed** form.* |
| | NO | TWO-SYLLABLE VERBS<br>(e) **ví**sit<br>**óf**fer | visiting<br>offering | visited<br>offered | If the first syllable of a two-syllable verb is stressed, do not double the consonant. |
| | YES | (f) pre**fér**<br>ad**mít** | preferring<br>admitting | preferred<br>admitted | If the second syllable of a two-syllable verb is stressed, double the consonant. |
| *-y* | NO | (g) pla**y**<br>enjo**y** | playing<br>enjoying | played<br>enjoyed | If the verb ends in a vowel + **-y**, keep the **-y**. Do not change the **-y** to **-i**. |
| | | (h) wor**ry**<br>stu**dy** | worrying<br>studying | worried<br>studied | If the verb ends in a consonant + **-y**, keep the **-y** for the **-ing** form, but change the **-y** to **-i** to make the **-ed** form. |
| *-ie* | | (i) die<br>tie | dying<br>tying | died<br>tied | **-ing** form: Change the **-ie** to **-y** and add **-ing**.<br>**-ed** form: Just add **-d**. |

*Exceptions: Do not double "w" or "x": *snow, snowing, snowed, fix, fixing, fixed.*

## 2-6 THE PRINCIPAL PARTS OF A VERB

|  | SIMPLE FORM | SIMPLE PAST | PAST PARTICIPLE | PRESENT PARTICIPLE |
|---|---|---|---|---|
| REGULAR VERBS | finish<br>stop<br>hope<br>wait<br>play<br>try | finished<br>stopped<br>hoped<br>waited<br>played<br>tried | finished<br>stopped<br>hoped<br>waited<br>played<br>tried | finishing<br>stopping<br>hoping<br>waiting<br>playing<br>trying |
| IRREGULAR VERBS | see<br>make<br>sing<br>eat<br>put<br>go | saw<br>made<br>sang<br>ate<br>put<br>went | seen<br>made<br>sung<br>eaten<br>put<br>gone | seeing<br>making<br>singing<br>eating<br>putting<br>going |
| PRINCIPAL PARTS OF A VERB<br>(1) the simple form | English verbs have four principal forms or "parts." **The simple form** is the form that is found in a dictionary. It is the base form with no endings on it (no final *-s*, *-ed*, or *-ing*). |
| (2) the simple past | **The simple past** form ends in *-ed* for regular verbs. Most verbs are regular, but many common verbs have irregular past forms. See the reference list of irregular verbs that follows in Chart 2-7. |
| (3) the past participle | **The past participle** also ends in *-ed* for regular verbs. Some verbs are irregular. It is used in perfect tenses (see Chapter 4) and the passive (Chapter 10). |
| (4) the present participle | **The present participle** ends in *-ing* (for both regular and irregular verbs). It is used in progressive tenses (e.g., the present progressive and the past progressive). |

My friend told me that he had a singing dog.
When the dog *sang*, I *put* my hands over my ears.

# 2-7 IRREGULAR VERBS: A REFERENCE LIST

| SIMPLE FORM | SIMPLE PAST | PAST PARTICIPLE | SIMPLE FORM | SIMPLE PAST | PAST PARTICIPLE |
|---|---|---|---|---|---|
| awake | awoke | awoken | lie | lay | lain |
| be | was, were | been | light | lit/lighted | lit/lighted |
| beat | beat | beaten | lose | lost | lost |
| become | became | become | make | made | made |
| begin | began | begun | mean | meant | meant |
| bend | bent | bent | meet | met | met |
| bite | bit | bitten | pay | paid | paid |
| blow | blew | blown | prove | proved | proved/proven |
| break | broke | broken | put | put | put |
| bring | brought | brought | quit | quit | quit |
| broadcast | broadcast | broadcast | read | read | read |
| build | built | built | ride | rode | ridden |
| burn | burned/burnt | burned/burnt | ring | rang | rung |
| buy | bought | bought | rise | rose | risen |
| catch | caught | caught | run | ran | run |
| choose | chose | chosen | say | said | said |
| come | came | come | see | saw | seen |
| cost | cost | cost | seek | sought | sought |
| cut | cut | cut | sell | sold | sold |
| dig | dug | dug | send | sent | sent |
| dive | dived/dove | dived | set | set | set |
| do | did | done | shake | shook | shaken |
| draw | drew | drawn | shave | shaved | shaved/shaven |
| dream | dreamed/dreamt | dreamed/dreamt | shoot | shot | shot |
| drink | drank | drunk | shut | shut | shut |
| drive | drove | driven | sing | sang | sung |
| eat | ate | eaten | sink | sank | sunk |
| fall | fell | fallen | sit | sat | sat |
| feed | fed | fed | sleep | slept | slept |
| feel | felt | felt | slide | slid | slid |
| fight | fought | fought | speak | spoke | spoken |
| find | found | found | spend | spent | spent |
| fit | fit | fit | spread | spread | spread |
| fly | flew | flown | stand | stood | stood |
| forget | forgot | forgotten | steal | stole | stolen |
| forgive | forgave | forgiven | stick | stuck | stuck |
| freeze | froze | frozen | strike | struck | struck |
| get | got | got/gotten | swear | swore | sworn |
| give | gave | given | sweep | swept | swept |
| go | went | gone | swim | swam | swum |
| grow | grew | grown | take | took | taken |
| hang | hung | hung | teach | taught | taught |
| have | had | had | tear | tore | torn |
| hear | heard | heard | tell | told | told |
| hide | hid | hidden | think | thought | thought |
| hit | hit | hit | throw | threw | thrown |
| hold | held | held | understand | understood | understood |
| hurt | hurt | hurt | upset | upset | upset |
| keep | kept | kept | wake | woke/waked | woken/waked |
| know | knew | known | wear | wore | worn |
| lay | laid | laid | weave | wove | woven |
| lead | led | led | weep | wept | wept |
| leave | left | left | win | won | won |
| lend | lent | lent | withdraw | withdrew | withdrawn |
| let | let | let | write | wrote | written |

## 2-8 THE SIMPLE PAST AND THE PAST PROGRESSIVE

| THE SIMPLE PAST | (a) Mary **walked** downtown yesterday. <br> (b) I **slept** for eight hours last night. | The SIMPLE PAST is used to talk about *an activity or situation that began and ended at a particular time in the past* (e.g., *yesterday, last night, two days ago, in 1999*), as in (a) and (b). |
|---|---|---|
| THE PAST PROGRESSIVE | (c) I sat down at the dinner table at 6:00 P.M. yesterday. Tom came to my house at 6:10 P.M. **I was eating** dinner *when Tom came.* <br> (d) I went to bed at 10:00. The phone rang at 11:00. **I was sleeping** *when the phone rang.* | The PAST PROGRESSIVE expresses *an activity that was in progress (was occurring, was happening)* at a point of time in the past (e.g., *at 6:10*) or at the time of another action (e.g., *when Tom came*). In (c): eating was in progress at 6:10; eating was in progress *when Tom came.* FORM: **was/were** + **-ing**. |
| (e) **When** *the phone rang,* I was sleeping. <br> (f) The phone rang **while** *I was sleeping.* | | **when** = at that time <br> **while** = during that time <br> (e) and (f) have the same meaning. |

## 2-9 FORMS OF THE PAST PROGRESSIVE

| STATEMENT | I-She-He-It **was working**. <br> You-We-They **were working**. | |
|---|---|---|
| NEGATIVE | I-She-He-It **was not (wasn't) working**. <br> You-We-They **were not (weren't) working**. | |
| QUESTION | **Was** I-she-he-it **working?** <br> **Were** you-we-they **working?** | |
| SHORT ANSWER | Yes, I-she-he-it **was**. <br> No, I-she-he-it **wasn't**. | Yes, you-we-they **were**. <br> No, you-we-they **weren't**. |

| | |
|---|---|
| (a) time clause *After I finished my work,* main clause *I went to bed.* | *After I finished my work* = a time clause★<br>*I went to bed* = a main clause★<br>(a) and (b) have the same meaning.<br>A time clause can<br>(1) come in front of a main clause, as in (a).<br>(2) follow a main clause, as in (b). |
| (b) main clause *I went to bed* time clause *after I finished my work.* | |
| (c) I went to bed ***after*** *I finished my work.*<br><br>(d) ***Before*** *I went to bed,* I finished my work.<br><br>(e) I stayed up ***until*** *I finished my work.*<br><br>(f) ***As soon as*** *I finished my work,* I went to bed.<br><br>(g) The phone rang ***while*** *I was watching* TV.<br><br>(h) ***When*** *the phone rang,* I was watching TV. | These words introduce time clauses:<br>**after**<br>**before**<br>**until**<br>**as soon as** } + *subject and verb* = a time clause<br>**while**<br>**when** |
| | In (e): *until* = "to that time and then no longer"★★<br>In (f): *as soon as* = "immediately after" |
| | PUNCTUATION: Put a comma at the end of a time clause when the time clause comes first in a sentence (comes in front of the main clause):<br>**time clause + comma + main clause**<br>**main clause + NO comma + time clause** |
| (i) When the phone ***rang***, I ***answered*** it. | In a sentence with a time clause introduced by *when*, both the time clause verb and the main verb can be simple past. In this case, the action in the *when-*clause happened first. In (i): *First: The phone rang. Then: I answered it.* |
| (j) While I ***was doing*** my homework, my roommate ***was watching*** TV. | In (j): When two actions are in progress at the same time, the past progressive can be used in both parts of the sentence. |

★A *clause* is a structure that has a subject and a verb.

★★***Until*** can also be used to say that something does NOT happen before a particular time: *I **didn't** go to bed **until** I finished my work.*

*When the phone rang,*
Susie ***answered*** it.

RING!
RING!

## 2-11 EXPRESSING PAST HABIT: *USED TO*

| | |
|---|---|
| (a) I **used to live** with my parents.  Now I live in my own apartment. <br> (b) Ann **used to be** afraid of dogs, but now she likes dogs. <br> (c) Al **used to smoke,** but he doesn't anymore. | **Used to** expresses a past situation or habit that no longer exists at present. <br><br> FORM: **used to** + *the simple form of a verb* |
| (d) **Did** you **used to** live in Paris? <br> (OR **Did** you **use to** live in Paris?) | QUESTION FORM: **did** + *subject* + **used to** <br> (OR **did** + *subject* + **use to**)* |
| (e) I **didn't used to** drink coffee at breakfast, but now I always have coffee in the morning. <br> (OR I **didn't use to** drink coffee.) <br> (f) I *never* **used to** drink coffee at breakfast, but now I always have coffee in the morning. | NEGATIVE FORM: **didn't used to** <br> (OR **didn't use to**)* <br> *Didn't use(d)* to occurs infrequently.  More commonly, people use *never* to express a negative idea with *used to*, as in (f). |

*Both forms (spelled *used to* or *use to* in questions and negatives) are possible.  There is no consensus among English language authorities on which is preferable.

Mr. Woods **used to have** a big dog.
Now he has a small dog.

# CHAPTER 3
## Future Time

## 3-1 EXPRESSING FUTURE TIME: *BE GOING TO* AND *WILL*

| FUTURE | (a) I **am going to leave** at nine tomorrow morning. <br> (b) I **will leave** at nine tomorrow morning. <br> (c) Marie **is going to be** at the meeting today.★ <br> (d) Marie **will be** at the meeting today. | *Be going to* and *will* are used to express future time. <br> (a) and (b) have the same meaning. <br> (c) and (d) have the same meaning. <br> *Will* and *be going to* often give the same meaning, but sometimes they express different meanings. The differences are discussed in Chart 3-5, p. 16. |
|---|---|---|
| (e) **I shall** leave at nine tomorrow morning. <br> (f) **We shall** leave at nine tomorrow morning. | | The use of *shall* (with *I* or *we*) to express future time is possible but infrequent. |

★*Today*, *tonight*, and *this* + *morning*, *afternoon*, *evening*, *week*, etc., can express present, past, or future time.

PRESENT: *Sam **is** in his office **this morning**.*

PAST: *Ann **was** in her office **this morning** at eight, but now she's at a meeting.*

FUTURE: *Bob **is going to be** in his office **this morning** after his dentist appointment.*

## 3-2 FORMS WITH *BE GOING TO*

| | |
|---|---|
| (a) We *are going to* **be** late.<br>(b) She's *going to* **come** tomorrow.<br>    *INCORRECT: She's going to comes tomorrow.* | ***Be going to*** is followed by the simple form of the verb, as in (a) and (b). |
| (c)  ***Am***    I<br>    ***Is***    he, she, it     } ***going to be*** late?<br>    ***Are***  they, we, you | QUESTION: ***be*** + *subject* + ***going to*** |
| (d)           I   ***am not***<br>   He, she, it  ***is not***    } ***going to be*** late.<br>  They, we, you  ***are not*** | NEGATIVE: ***be*** + ***not*** + ***going to*** |
| (e) "Hurry up! We're ***gonna*** be late!" | ***Be going to*** is more common in speaking and in informal writing than in formal writing. In informal speaking, it is sometimes pronounced "gonna" /gənə/.<br>"Gonna" is not usually a written form. |

## 3-3 FORMS WITH *WILL*

| | |
|---|---|
| STATEMENT | I-You-She-He-It-We-They ***will come*** tomorrow. |
| NEGATIVE | I-You-She-He-It-We-They ***will not (won't) come*** tomorrow. |
| QUESTION | ***Will*** I-you-she-he-it-we-they ***come*** tomorrow? |
| SHORT ANSWER | Yes,<br>No,  } I-you-she-he-it-we-they  {***will.*** ★<br>                                        {***won't.*** |
| CONTRACTIONS | *I'll*      *she'll*    *we'll*<br>*you'll*    *he'll*     *they'll*<br>           *it'll* | ***Will*** is usually contracted with pronouns in both speech and informal writing. |
| | Bob + ***will*** = "Bob***'ll***"<br>the teacher + ***will*** = "the teacher***'ll***" | ***Will*** is often contracted with nouns in speech, but usually not in writing. |

★Pronouns are NOT contracted with helping verbs in short answers.
    *CORRECT: Yes, I will.*
    *INCORRECT: Yes, I'll.*

## 3-4 SURENESS ABOUT THE FUTURE

| 100% sure | (a) I **will be** in class tomorrow. OR<br>I **am going to be** in class tomorrow. | In (a): The speaker uses **will** or **be going to** because he feels sure about his future activity. He is stating a fact about the future. |
|---|---|---|
| 90% sure | (b) Po **will probably be** in class tomorrow. OR<br>Po **is probably going to be** in class tomorrow.<br>(c) Anna **probably won't be** in class tomorrow. OR<br>Anna **probably isn't going to be** in class tomorrow. | In (b): The speaker uses **probably** to say that he expects Po to be in class tomorrow, but he is not 100% sure. He's almost sure, but not completely sure.<br>Word order with **probably:**\*<br>(1) in a statement, as in (b):<br>*helping verb* + **probably**<br>(2) with a negative verb, as in (c):<br>**probably** + *helping verb* |
| 50% sure | (d) Ali **may come** to class tomorrow, or Ali **may not come** to class tomorrow. I don't know what he's going to do. | **May** expresses a future possibility: maybe something will happen, and maybe it won't happen.\*\* In (d): The speaker is saying that maybe Ali will come to class, or maybe he won't come to class. The speaker is guessing. |
|  | (e) **Maybe** Ali **will come** to class, and **maybe** he **won't**. OR<br>**Maybe** Ali **is going to come** to class, and **maybe** he **isn't**. | **Maybe** + **will**/**be going to** gives the same meaning as **may**. (d) and (e) have the same meaning.<br>**Maybe** comes at the beginning of a sentence. |

\*See Chart 1-3, p. 3, for more information about placement of midsentence adverbs such as **probably**.
\*\*See Chart 7-3, p. 50, for more information about **may**.

## 3-5 *BE GOING TO* vs. *WILL*

| (a) She **is going to succeed** because she works hard.<br>(b) She **will succeed** because she works hard. | **Be going to** and **will** mean the same when they are used to make predictions about the future.<br>(a) and (b) have the same meaning. |
|---|---|
| (c) I bought some wood because I **am going to build** a bookcase for my apartment. | **Be going to** (but not **will**) is used to express a prior plan (i.e., a plan made before the moment of speaking). In (c): The speaker plans to build a bookcase. |
| (d) This chair is too heavy for you to carry alone. I**'ll help** you. | **Will** (but not **be going to**) is used to express a decision the speaker makes at the moment of speaking. In (d): The speaker decides to help at the immediate present moment; he did not have a prior plan or intention to help. |

## 3-6 EXPRESSING THE FUTURE IN TIME CLAUSES AND *IF*-CLAUSES

| | |
|---|---|
| (a) \|**Before I go** *to class tomorrow*\| , I'm going to eat breakfast. <br><br>(b) I'm going to eat breakfast \|**before I go** *to class tomorrow.*\| | In (a) and (b): *before I go to class tomorrow* is a future time clause. <br><br>$\left.\begin{array}{l}\textbf{\textit{before}} \\ \textbf{\textit{after}} \\ \textbf{\textit{when}} \\ \textbf{\textit{as soon as}} \\ \textbf{\textit{until}} \\ \textbf{\textit{while}}\end{array}\right\}$ + *subject and verb* = a time clause |
| (c) *Before I* **go** *home tonight,* I'm going to stop at the market. <br><br>(d) I'm going to eat dinner at 6:00 tonight. *After I* **eat** *dinner,* I'm going to study in my room. <br><br>(e) I'll give Rita your message *when I* **see** *her.* <br><br>(f) It's raining right now. *As soon as the rain* **stops**, I'm going to walk downtown. <br><br>(g) I'll stay home *until the rain* **stops**. <br><br>(h) *While you're* *at school tomorrow,* I'll be at work. | The simple present is used in a future time clause. **Will** and **be going to** are NOT used in a future time clause. <br><br>INCORRECT: *Before I will go to class, I'm going to eat breakfast.* <br><br>INCORRECT: *Before I am going to go to class tomorrow, I'm going to eat breakfast.* <br><br>All of the example sentences, (c) through (h), contain future time clauses. |
| (i) Maybe it will rain tomorrow. *If it* **rains** *tomorrow,* I'm going to stay home. | In (i): *If it rains tomorrow* is an *if*-clause. <br>*if* + *subject and verb* = an *if*-clause <br>When the meaning is future, the simple present (not **will** or **be going to**) is used in an *if*-clause. |

## 3-7 USING THE PRESENT PROGRESSIVE TO EXPRESS FUTURE TIME

| | |
|---|---|
| (a) Tom **is going to come** to the party tomorrow. <br>(b) Tom **is coming** to the party tomorrow. <br>(c) We**'re going to go** to a movie tonight. <br>(d) We**'re going** to a movie tonight. <br>(e) I**'m going to stay** home this evening. <br>(f) I**'m staying** home this evening. <br>(g) Ann **is going to fly** to Chicago next week. <br>(h) Ann **is flying** to Chicago next week. | The present progressive can be used to express future time. Each pair of example sentences has the same meaning. <br><br>The present progressive describes *definite plans for the future, plans that were made before the moment of speaking.* |
| | A future meaning for the present progressive is indicated either by future time words (e.g., *tomorrow*) or by the situation.★ |
| (i) You**'re going to laugh** when you hear this joke. <br>(j) INCORRECT: *You're laughing when you hear this joke.* | The present progressive is NOT used for predictions about the future. In (i): The speaker is predicting a future event. In (j): The present progressive is not possible; laughing is a prediction, not a planned future event. |

★COMPARE: Present situation: *Look! Mary's coming. Do you see her?*
Future situation: *Are you planning to come to the party? Mary's coming. So is Alex.*

## 3-8 USING THE SIMPLE PRESENT TO EXPRESS FUTURE TIME

| | |
|---|---|
| (a) My plane **arrives** at 7:35 *tomorrow evening.*<br>(b) Tom's new job **starts** *next week.*<br>(c) The semester **ends** *in two more weeks.*<br>(d) There **is** a meeting at ten *tomorrow morning.* | The simple present can express future time when events are on a definite schedule or timetable. Only a few verbs are used in the simple present to express future time. The most common are ***arrive, leave, start, begin, end, finish, open, close, be.*** |
| (e) INCORRECT: *I wear my new suit to the wedding next week.*<br>CORRECT: *I am wearing/am going to wear* my new suit to the wedding next week. | Most verbs **cannot** be used in the simple present to express future time. For example, in (e): The verb ***wear*** does not express an event on a schedule or timetable. It cannot be used in the simple present to express future time. |

## 3-9 IMMEDIATE FUTURE: USING *BE ABOUT TO*

| | |
|---|---|
| (a) Ann's bags are packed, and she is wearing her coat. She **is about to leave** for the airport.<br>(b) Shhh. The movie **is about to begin**. | The idiom "be about to do something" expresses an activity that will happen *in the immediate future,* usually within minutes or seconds. In (a): Ann is going to leave sometime in the next few minutes. |

## 3-10 PARALLEL VERBS

| | |
|---|---|
| (a) Jim   <sub>v</sub>**makes** his bed <sub>and</sub>*and* <sub>v</sub>**cleans** up his room every morning. | Often a subject has two verbs that are connected by ***and***. We say that the two verbs are parallel:<br>    v + ***and*** + v<br>    *makes and cleans* = parallel verbs |
| (b) Ann **is cooking** dinner *and (is)* **talking** on the phone at the same time.<br>(c) I **will stay** home and *(will)* **study** tonight.<br>(d) I **am going to stay** home and *(am going to)* **study** tonight. | It is not necessary to repeat a helping verb (an auxiliary verb) when two verbs are connected by ***and***. |

# CHAPTER *4*

## The Present Perfect and the Past Perfect

## 4-1 PAST PARTICIPLE

| | SIMPLE FORM | SIMPLE PAST | PAST PARTICIPLE | The **past participle** is one of the principal parts of a verb. (See Chart 2-6, p. 9.) |
|---|---|---|---|---|
| REGULAR VERBS | finish<br>stop<br>wait | finished<br>stopped<br>waited | **finished**<br>**stopped**<br>**waited** | The past participle is used in the PRESENT PERFECT tense and the PAST PERFECT tense.*<br>The past participle of regular verbs is the same as the simple past form: both end in *-ed*. |
| IRREGULAR VERBS | see<br>make<br>put | saw<br>made<br>put | **seen**<br>**made**<br>**put** | See Chart 2-7, p. 10, for a list of irregular verbs. |

*The past participle is also used in the passive. See Chapter 10.

The bee is resting. It **has finished** its work.

| | |
|---|---|
| (a) I **have finished** my work. <br> (b) The students **have finished** Chapter 3. <br> (c) Jim **has eaten** lunch. | STATEMENT: **have/has** + *past participle* |
| (d) **I've/You've/We've/They've** *eaten* lunch. <br> (e) **She's/He's** *eaten* lunch. <br> (f) **It's** *been* cold for the last three days. | CONTRACTION <br> *pronoun* + **have** = **'ve** <br> *pronoun* + **has** = **'s**★ |
| (g) I **have not (haven't) finished** my work. <br> (h) Ann **has not (hasn't) eaten** lunch. | NEGATIVE: **have/has** + **not** + *past participle* <br> NEGATIVE CONTRACTION <br>     **have** + **not** = **haven't** <br>     **has** + **not** = **hasn't** |
| (i) **Have you finished** your work? <br> (j) **Has Jim eaten** lunch? <br> (k) How long **have you lived** here? | QUESTION: **have/has** + *subject* + *past participle* |
| (l) A: Have you seen that movie? <br>     B: *Yes, I* **have.** OR *No, I* **haven't.** <br> (m) A: Has Jim eaten lunch? <br>     B: *Yes, he* **has.** OR *No, he* **hasn't.** | SHORT ANSWER: **have/haven't** or **has/hasn't** <br> Note: The helping verb in the short answer is not contracted with the pronoun. <br> *INCORRECT: Yes, I've.* OR *Yes, he's.* |

    ★COMPARE: **It's** cold today. [*It's* = *It is:* **It is** *cold today.*]

        **It's** been cold since December. [*It's* = *It has:* **It has** *been cold since December.*]

**Have you ever gone** to a costume party?

Jim has eaten lunch.        Ann hasn't eaten lunch.

**PRESENT PERFECT, MEANING #1: SOMETHING HAPPENED BEFORE NOW AT AN UNSPECIFIED TIME.**

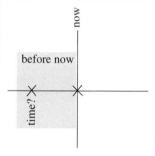

(a) Jim **has** already **eaten** lunch.
(b) Ann **hasn't eaten** lunch yet.
(c) **Have** you ever **eaten** at that restaurant?

The PRESENT PERFECT expresses an activity or situation that occurred (or did not occur) *before now, at some unspecified time in the past.*
In (a): Jim's lunch occurred before the present time. The exact time is not mentioned; it is unimportant or unknown. For the speaker, the only important information is that Jim's lunch occurred in the past, sometime before now.

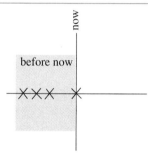

(d) Pete **has eaten** at that restaurant *many times.*
(e) I **have eaten** there *twice.*

An activity may be repeated two, several, or more times *before now,* at *unspecified times in the past,* as in (d) and (e).

**PRESENT PERFECT, MEANING #2: A SITUATION BEGAN IN THE PAST AND CONTINUES TO THE PRESENT.**

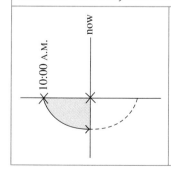

(f) We**'ve been** in class *since ten o'clock this morning.*
(g) I **have known** Ben *for ten years.* I met him ten years ago. I still know him today. We are friends.

When the present perfect is used with *since* or *for,* it expresses situations that began in the past and continue to the present.
In (f): Class started at ten. We are still in class now, at the moment of speaking.
*INCORRECT: We are in class since ten o'clock this morning.*

## 4-4 SIMPLE PAST vs. PRESENT PERFECT

| | |
|---|---|
| SIMPLE PAST<br>(a) I *finished* my work *two hours ago.*<br><br>PRESENT PERFECT<br>(b) I *have* already\* *finished* my work. | In (a): I finished my work at a specific time in the past *(two hours ago).*<br>In (b): I finished my work at an unspecified time in the past *(sometime before now).*<br>The SIMPLE PAST expresses an activity that occurred at a specific time (or times) in the past, as in (a) and (c).<br>The PRESENT PERFECT expresses an activity that occurred at an unspecified time (or times) in the past, as in (b) and (d). |
| SIMPLE PAST<br>(c) I *was* in Europe *last year/three years ago/in 1999/in 1995 and 1999/when I was ten years old.*<br><br>PRESENT PERFECT<br>(d) I *have been* in Europe *many times/several times/a couple of times/once/(no mention of time).* | |
| SIMPLE PAST<br>(e) Ann *was* in Miami *for two weeks.*<br><br>PRESENT PERFECT<br>(f) Bob *has been* in Miami *for two weeks/since May first.* | In (e): In sentences where *for* is used in a time expression, the simple past expresses an activity that began and ended in the past.<br>In (f): In sentences with *for* or *since,* the present perfect expresses an activity that began in the past and continues to the present. |

\*For more information about *already,* see Chart 4-8, p. 26.

Grandpa has a brand new bicycle.
It is not his first bicycle.
In his lifetime, he *has owned* several bicycles.

| SINCE | | | |
|---|---|---|---|
| | (a) I **have been** here | **since** eight o'clock.<br>**since** Tuesday.<br>**since** May.<br>**since** 1999.<br>**since** January 3, 2001.<br>**since** yesterday.<br>**since** last month. | ***Since*** is followed by the mention of *a specific point in time:* an hour, a day, a month, a year, etc.<br>***Since*** expresses the idea that something began at a specific time in the past and continues to the present. |
| | (b)   CORRECT:  I ***have lived*** here since May.*<br>        CORRECT:  I ***have been*** here since May.<br>(c) *INCORRECT:*  *I am living here since May.*<br>(d) *INCORRECT:*  *I live here since May.*<br>(e) *INCORRECT:*  *I lived here since May.*<br>       *INCORRECT:*  *I was here since May.* | | The *present perfect* is used in sentences with **since**.<br>In (c): The present progressive is NOT used.<br>In (d): The simple present is NOT used.<br>In (e): The simple past is NOT used. |
| |     MAIN CLAUSE<br>    (present perfect)<br>(f) I ***have lived*** here<br>(g) Al ***has met*** many people |   SINCE-CLAUSE<br>  (simple past)<br>since I ***was*** a child.<br>since he ***came*** here. | ***Since*** may also introduce a time clause (i.e., a subject and verb may follow ***since***).<br>Notice in the examples: The present perfect is used in the main clause; the simple past is used in the ***since***-clause. |
| FOR | (h) I ***have been*** here | **for** ten minutes.<br>**for** two hours.<br>**for** five days.<br>**for** about three weeks.<br>**for** almost six months.<br>**for** many years.<br>**for** a long time. | ***For*** is followed by the mention of a *length of time:* two minutes, three hours, four days, five weeks, etc.<br>Note: If the noun ends in **-s** *(hours, days, weeks, etc.)*, use ***for*** in the time expression, not ***since***. |
| | (i) I ***have lived*** here ***for*** *two years.*  I moved here two years ago, and I still live here.<br>(j) I ***lived*** in Athens ***for*** *two years.*  I don't live in Athens now. | | In (i): The use of the present perfect in a sentence with ***for*** + *a length of time* means that the action began in the past and continues to the present.<br>In (j): The use of the simple past means that the action began and ended in the past. |

*ALSO CORRECT: *I **have been living** here since May.*  See Chart 4-7, p. 25, for a discussion of the present perfect progressive.

| | |
|---|---|
| Al and Ann are in their car right now. They are driving home. It is now four o'clock. | The PRESENT PERFECT PROGRESSIVE talks about *how long* an activity has been in progress before now. |
| (a) They *have been driving* since two o'clock. | Note: Time expressions with *since*, as in (a), and *for*, as in (b), are frequently used with this tense. |
| (b) They *have been driving* for two hours. They will be home soon. | STATEMENT: *have/has* + *been* + *-ing* |
| (c) How long *have they been driving*? | QUESTION FORM: *have/has* + *subject* + *been* + *-ing* |

COMPARE the present progressive and the present perfect progressive.

| PRESENT PROGRESSIVE 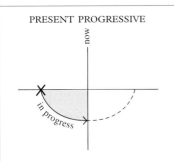 | (d) Po *is sitting* in class right now. | The PRESENT PROGRESSIVE describes an activity that is in progress right now, as in (d). It does not discuss duration (length of time). *INCORRECT: Po has been sitting in class right now.* |
|---|---|---|
| PRESENT PERFECT PROGRESSIVE 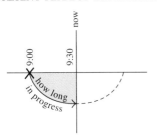 | Po is sitting at his desk in class. He sat down at nine o'clock. It is now nine-thirty. (e) Po *has been sitting* in class *since* nine o'clock. (f) Po *has been sitting* in class *for* thirty minutes. | The PRESENT PERFECT PROGRESSIVE expresses the **duration** (length of time) of an activity that began in the past and is in progress right now. *INCORRECT: Po is sitting in class since nine o'clock.* |

| | |
|---|---|
| (g)  CORRECT:  I *know* Yoko. | Reminder: Non-action verbs (e.g., *know, like, own, belong*) are not used in any progressive tenses.* |
| (h)  *INCORRECT*:  I *am knowing* Yoko. | In (i): With non-action verbs, the present perfect is used with *since* or *for* to express the duration of a |
| (i)  CORRECT:  I *have known* Yoko *for* two years. | situation that began in the past and continues to the present. |
| (j)  *INCORRECT*:  I *have been knowing* Yoko for two years. | |

*See Chart 1-6 (Non-Action Verbs), p. 5.

## 4-7 PRESENT PERFECT PROGRESSIVE vs. PRESENT PERFECT

| | |
|---|---|
| PRESENT PERFECT PROGRESSIVE<br>(a) Rita and Josh are talking on the phone.<br>They ***have been talking*** on the phone for twenty minutes. | The PRESENT PERFECT PROGRESSIVE expresses the **duration of present *activities*** that are in progress, using action verbs, as in (a). |
| PRESENT PERFECT<br>(b) Rita ***has talked*** to Josh on the phone many times (before now).<br>(c) INCORRECT: *Rita has been talking to Josh on the phone many times.*<br>(d) Rita ***has known*** Josh for two years.<br>(e) INCORRECT: *Rita has been knowing Josh for two years.* | The PRESENT PERFECT expresses<br>(1) repeated activities that occur at **unspecified times in the past**, as in (b), or<br><br>(2) the **duration of present *situations***, as in (d), using non-action verbs. |
| (f) I ***have been living*** here for six months. OR<br>(g) I ***have lived*** here for six months.<br><br>(h) Al ***has been wearing*** glasses since he was ten. OR<br>Al ***has worn*** glasses since he was ten.<br><br>(i) I'***ve been going*** to school ever since I was five years old. OR<br>I'***ve gone*** to school ever since I was five years old. | For some (not all) verbs, duration can be expressed by either the present perfect or the present perfect progressive. (f) and (g) have essentially the same meaning, and both are correct.<br>Often either tense can be used with verbs that express the **duration of usual or habitual activities/situations** (things that happen daily or regularly), e.g., *live, work, teach, smoke, wear glasses, play chess, go to school, read the same newspaper every morning,* etc. |

## 4-8 USING *ALREADY, YET, STILL,* AND *ANYMORE*

| ALREADY | (a) The mail came an hour ago. **The mail is *already* here.** | Idea of *already:* Something happened before now, before this time. *Position: midsentence.*★ |
|---|---|---|
| YET | (b) I expected the mail an hour ago, but **it hasn't come *yet*.** | Idea of *yet:* Something did not happen before now (up to this time), but it may happen in the future. *Position: end of sentence.* |
| STILL | (c) It was cold yesterday. **It is *still* cold** today. **We *still* need to wear coats.** (d) I could play the piano when I was a child. **I can *still* play the piano.** (e) The mail didn't come an hour ago. **The mail *still* hasn't come.** | Idea of *still:* A situation continues to exist from past to present without change. *Position: midsentence.*★ |
| ANYMORE | (f) I lived in Chicago two years ago, but then I moved to another city. **I don't live in Chicago *anymore*.** | Idea of *anymore:* A past situation does not continue to exist at present; a past situation has changed. ***Anymore* has the same meaning as *any longer*.** *Position: end of sentence.* |

Note: ***Already*** is used in *affirmative* sentences.
      ***Yet*** and ***anymore*** are used in *negative* sentences.
      ***Still*** is used in either *affirmative or negative* sentences.

★See Chart 1-3, p. 3. A midsentence adverb
    (1) precedes a simple present verb: *We **still** need to wear coats.*
    (2) follows *am, is, are, was, were: It **is still** cold.*
    (3) comes between a helping verb and a main verb: *Bob **has already** arrived.*
    (4) precedes a negative helping verb: *Ann **still hasn't** come.*
    (5) follows the subject in a question: *Have **you already** seen that movie?*

The children are ***still*** working on their sand castle.
They haven't finished it ***yet***.

*Situation: Jack left his apartment at 2:00. Ann arrived at his apartment at 2:15 and knocked on the door.*

(a) When Ann arrived, Jack wasn't there. He **had left**.

The PAST PERFECT is used when the speaker is talking about two different events at two different times in the past; one event ends before the second event happens.

In (a): There are two events, and both happened in the past: *Jack left his apartment. Ann arrived at his apartment.* To show the time relationship between the two events, we use the past perfect *(had left)* to say that the first event (Jack leaving his apartment) was completed before the second event (Ann arriving at his apartment) occurred.

(continued)

| | |
|---|---|
| (b) Jack **had left** his apartment when Ann arrived. | FORM: **had** + *past participle* |
| (c) *He'd* left. *I'd* left. *They'd* left. Etc. | CONTRACTION:<br>*I/you/she/he/it/we/they* + **'d** |

COMPARE THE PRESENT PERFECT AND THE PAST PERFECT.

| PRESENT PERFECT | (d) I am not hungry now. I *have* already *eaten*. | The PRESENT PERFECT expresses an activity that *occurred before now, at an unspecified time in the past*, as in (d). |
|---|---|---|
| before now / now | | |
| PAST PERFECT | (e) I was not hungry at 1:00 P.M. I *had* already *eaten*. | The PAST PERFECT expresses an activity that *occurred before another time in the past.*<br>In (e): I ate at noon. I was not hungry at 1:00 P.M. because I had already eaten before 1:00 P.M. |
| before 1:00 / 1:00 P.M. | | |

COMPARE THE PAST PROGRESSIVE AND THE PAST PERFECT.

| PAST PROGRESSIVE | (f) I *was eating* when Bob came. | The PAST PROGRESSIVE expresses an activity that was *in progress at a particular time in the past.*<br>In (f): I began to eat at noon. Bob came at 12:10. My meal was in progress when Bob came. |
|---|---|---|
| began eating / Bob came / eating in progress | | |
| PAST PERFECT | (g) I *had eaten* when Bob came. | The PAST PERFECT expresses an activity that was *completed before a particular time in the past.*<br>In (g): I finished eating at noon. Bob came at 1:00 P.M. My meal was completed before Bob came. |
| finished eating / Bob came | | |

# CHAPTER 5
# Asking Questions

## CONTENTS

## 5-1   YES/NO QUESTIONS AND SHORT ANSWERS

| YES/NO QUESTION | SHORT ANSWER (+ LONG ANSWER) |
|---|---|
| (a) **Do** *you* **like** tea? | *Yes, I do*. (I like tea.) <br> *No, I don't*. (I don't like tea.) |
| (b) **Did** *Sue* **call**? | *Yes, she did*. (Sue called.) <br> *No, she didn't*. (Sue didn't call.) |
| (c) **Have** *you* **met** Al? | *Yes, I have*. (I have met Al.) <br> *No, I haven't*. (I haven't met Al.) |
| (d) **Is** *it* **raining**? | *Yes, it is*. (It's raining.) <br> *No, it isn't*. (It isn't raining.) |
| (e) **Will** *Rob* **be** here? | *Yes, he will*. (Rob will be here.) <br> *No, he won't*. (Rob won't be here.) |

A **yes/no question** is a question that can be answered by *yes* or *no*.

In an affirmative short answer (yes), a helping verb is NOT contracted with the subject.

In (c): *INCORRECT: Yes, I've.*
In (d): *INCORRECT: Yes, it's.*
In (e): *INCORRECT: Yes, he'll.*

The spoken emphasis in a short answer is on the verb.

## 5-2 YES/NO QUESTIONS AND INFORMATION QUESTIONS

A yes/no question = a question that can be answered by "yes" or "no."
> A: *Does Ann live in Montreal?*
> B: *Yes, she does.* OR *No, she doesn't.*

An information question = a question that asks for information by using a question word: ***where, when, why, who, whom, what, which, whose, how.***
> A: *Where does Ann live?*
> B: *In Montreal.*

| | (QUESTION WORD) | HELPING VERB | SUBJECT | MAIN VERB | (REST OF SENTENCE) | The same subject-verb word order is used in both yes/no and information questions. |
|---|---|---|---|---|---|---|
| (a) | | ***Does*** | *Ann* | ***live*** | in Montreal? | HELPING VERB + SUBJECT + MAIN VERB |
| (b) | Where | *does* | *Ann* | *live?* | | |
| (c) | | ***Is*** | *Sara* | ***studying*** | at the library? | (a) is a yes/no question. |
| (d) | Where | *is* | *Sara* | ***studying?*** | | (b) is an information question. |
| (e) | | ***Will*** | *you* | ***graduate*** | next year? | In (i) and (j): Main verb ***be*** in simple present and simple past (***am, is, are, was, were***) precedes the subject. It has the same position as a helping verb. |
| (f) | When | ***will*** | *you* | ***graduate?*** | | |
| (g) | | ***Did*** | *they* | ***see*** | Jack? | |
| (h) | Who(m)* | ***did*** | *they* | ***see?*** | | |
| (i) | | ***Is*** | *Heidi* | | at home? | |
| (j) | Where | ***is*** | *Heidi?* | | | |
| (k) | | | *Who* | ***came*** | to dinner? | When the question word (e.g., ***who*** or ***what***) is the subject of the question, usual question word order is not used. No form of ***do*** is used. Notice (k) and (l). |
| (l) | | | *What* | ***happened*** | yesterday? | |

*See Chart 5-4, p. 31, for a discussion of ***who(m)***.

## 5-3 *WHERE, WHY, WHEN,* AND *WHAT TIME*

| QUESTION | ANSWER | |
|---|---|---|
| (a) ***Where*** did you go? | Paris. | ***Where*** asks about *place*. |
| (b) ***Why*** did you stay home? | Because I didn't feel well.* | ***Why*** asks about *reason*. |
| (c) ***What time*** did he come? | Seven-thirty.<br>Around five o'clock.<br>A quarter past ten. | A question with ***what time*** asks about *time on a clock*. |
| (d) ***When*** did he come? | Seven-thirty.<br>Last night.<br>Two days ago.<br>Monday morning.<br>In 1998. | A question with ***when*** can be answered by any time expression, as in the sample answers in (d). |

*See Chart 8-6, p. 59, for the use of *because*. "Because I didn't feel well" is an adverb clause. It is not a complete sentence. In this example, it is the short answer to a question.

## 5-4 QUESTIONS WITH *WHO, WHO(M)*, AND *WHAT*

| QUESTION | ANSWER | |
|---|---|---|
| (a) **Who** came? (s) | **Someone** came. (s) | In (a): **Who** is used as the subject (s) of a question. In (b): **Who(m)** is used as the object (o) in a question. **Whom** is used in formal English. In everyday spoken English, **who** is usually used instead of **whom**:<br>FORMAL: Whom did you see?<br>INFORMAL: Who did you see? |
| (b) **Who(m)** did *you* see? (o) | *I* saw **someone**. (s) (o) | |
| (c) **What** happened? (s) | **Something** happened. (s) | **What** can be used as either the subject or the object in a question. Notice in (a) and (c): When **who** or **what** is used as the subject of a question, usual question word order is not used; no form of **do** is used:<br>CORRECT: Who came?<br>*INCORRECT: Who did come?* |
| (d) **What** did *you* see? (o) | *I* saw **something**. (s) (o) | |

## 5-5 SPOKEN AND WRITTEN CONTRACTIONS WITH QUESTION WORDS

| | | SPOKEN ONLY | | |
|---|---|---|---|---|
| **is** | (a) | "*When's* he coming?"<br>"*Why's* she late?" | | **Is, are, did**, and **will** are usually contracted with question words in speaking. These contractions are usually NOT written. |
| **are** | (b) | "*What're* these?"<br>"*Who're* they?" | | |
| **did** | (c) | "*Who'd* you see?"<br>"*What'd* you do?" | | |
| **will** | (d) | "*Where'll* you be?"<br>"*When'll* they be here?" | | |
| | | SPOKEN | WRITTEN | |
| **is** | (e) | "*Where's* Ed?"<br>"*What's* that?"<br>"*Who's* he?" | (f) Where's Ed?<br>What's that?<br>Who's he? | Only contractions with **is** and **where, what**, or **who** are commonly used in writing.* |

*Contractions are used in informal writing, such as letters to friends or e-mails, but are generally not appropriate in more formal writing, such as in magazine articles or reference books.

## 5-6 USING *WHAT* + A FORM OF *DO*

| QUESTION | ANSWER | |
|---|---|---|
| (a) *What **does** Bob **do** every morning?* | He *goes to class.* | ***What*** + a form of ***do*** is used to ask questions about activities. Examples of forms of ***do***: *am doing, will do, are going to do, did, etc.* |
| (b) *What **did** you **do** yesterday?* | I *went downtown.* | |
| (c) *What **is** Anna **doing** (right now)?* | She*'s studying.* | |
| (d) *What **are** you **going to do** tomorrow?* | I*'m going to go to the beach.* | |
| (e) *What **do** you **want to do** tonight?* | I *want to go to a movie.* | |
| (f) *What **would** you **like to do** tomorrow?* | I *would like to visit Jim.* | |
| (g) *What **will** you **do** tomorrow?* | I*'ll go downtown.* | |
| (h) *What **should** I **do** about my headache?* | You *should take an aspirin.* | |

## 5-7 USING *WHAT KIND OF*

| QUESTION | ANSWER | |
|---|---|---|
| (a) ***What kind of*** *shoes did you buy?* | Boots.<br>Sandals.<br>Tennis shoes.<br>Loafers.<br>Running shoes.<br>High heels.<br>Etc. | ***What kind of*** asks for information about a specific type (a specific kind) in a general category.<br><br>In (a):<br>general category = shoes<br>specific kinds = boots<br>　　　　　　　sandals<br>　　　　　　　tennis shoes<br>　　　　　　　etc. |

| QUESTION | ANSWER | |
|---|---|---|
| (b) ***What kind of*** *fruit do you like best?* | Apples.<br>Bananas.<br>Oranges.<br>Grapefruit.<br>Grapes.<br>Strawberries.<br>Etc. | In (b):<br>general category = fruit<br>specific kinds = apples<br>　　　　　　　bananas<br>　　　　　　　oranges<br>　　　　　　　etc. |

## 5-8 USING *WHICH*

| | |
|---|---|
| (a) TOM: May I borrow a pen from you?<br>ANN: Sure.  I have two pens.  This pen has black ink.<br>That pen has red ink.<br>***Which pen***   do you want?   OR<br>***Which one***   do you want?   OR<br>***Which***        do you want? | In (a): Ann uses ***which*** (not ***what***) because she wants Tom to choose.<br>***Which*** is used when the speaker wants someone to make a choice, when the speaker is offering alternatives: *this one or that one; these or those.* |
| (b) SUE: I like these earrings, and I like those, too.<br>BOB: ***Which (earrings/ones)*** are you going to buy?<br>SUE: I think I'll get these. | ***Which*** can be used with either singular or plural nouns. |
| (c) JIM: Here's a photo of my daughter's class.<br>KIM: Very nice.  ***Which one*** is your daughter? | ***Which*** can be used to ask about people as well as things. |
| (d) SUE: My aunt gave me some money for my birthday.<br>I'm going to take it with me to the mall.<br>BOB: ***What*** are you going to buy with it?<br>SUE: I haven't decided yet. | In (d): The question doesn't involve choosing from a particular group of items, so Bob uses ***what***, not ***which***. |

***Which*** *tie* is he going to buy?

## 5-9 USING *WHOSE*

| QUESTION | ANSWER | |
|---|---|---|
| (a) ***Whose (book)*** is this?<br>(b) ***Whose (books)*** are those?<br>(c) ***Whose car*** did you borrow? | It's John's (book).<br>They're mine (OR my books).<br>I borrowed Karen's (car). | ***Whose*** asks about possession.*<br>Notice in (a): The speaker of the question may omit the noun *(book)* if the meaning is clear to the listener. |
| COMPARE<br>(d) ***Who's*** that?<br>(e) ***Whose*** is that? | Mary Smith.<br>Mary's. | ***Who's*** and ***whose*** have the same pronunciation.<br>***Who's*** = a contraction of ***who is***.<br>***Whose*** = asks about possession. |

*See Charts 6-11 and 6-12, p. 45, for ways of expressing possession.

## 5-10 USING *HOW*

| QUESTION | ANSWER | |
|---|---|---|
| (a) **How** did you get here? | I drove./By car.<br>I took a taxi./By taxi.<br>I took a bus./By bus.<br>I flew./By plane.<br>I took a train./By train.<br>I walked./On foot. | **How** has many uses. One use of **how** is to ask about means (ways) of transportation. |
| (b) **How old** are you?<br>(c) **How tall** is he?<br>(d) **How big** is your apartment?<br>(e) **How sleepy** are you?<br>(f) **How hungry** are you?<br>(g) **How soon** will you be ready?<br>(h) **How well** does he speak English?<br>(i) **How quickly** can you get here? | Twenty-one.<br>About six feet.<br>It has three rooms.<br>Very sleepy.<br>I'm starving.<br>In five minutes.<br>Very well.<br>I can get there in 30 minutes. | **How** is often used with adjectives (e.g., *old, big*) and adverbs (e.g., *well, quickly*). |

## 5-11 USING *HOW OFTEN*

| QUESTION | ANSWER | |
|---|---|---|
| (a) **How often** do you go shopping? | Every day.<br>Once a week.<br>About twice a week.<br>Every other day or so.★<br>Three times a month. | **How often** asks about frequency. |
| (b) **How many times a day** do you eat?<br>**How many times a week** do you go shopping?<br>**How many times a month** do you go to the post office?<br>**How many times a year** do you take a vacation? | Three or four.<br><br>Two.<br><br>Once.<br><br>Once or twice. | Other ways of asking **how often**:<br><br>**how many times** { *a day*<br>*a week*<br>*a month*<br>*a year* |

★*Every other day* means "Monday yes, Tuesday no, Wednesday yes, Thursday no," etc. *Or so* means "approximately."

## 5-12 USING *HOW FAR*

| | |
|---|---|
| (a) *It is* 289 miles *from* St. Louis *to* Chicago.* <br><br> (b) *It is* 289 miles { *from* St. Louis *to* Chicago. <br> *from* Chicago *to* St. Louis. <br> *to* Chicago *from* St. Louis. <br> *to* St. Louis *from* Chicago. | The most common way of expressing distance: <br> *It is* + *distance* + *from*/*to* + *to*/*from* <br> In (b): All four expressions with *from* and *to* have the same meaning. |
| (c) A: *How far is it* from St. Louis to Chicago? <br>     B: 289 miles. <br> (d) A: *How far do you* live from school? <br>     B: Four blocks. | *How far* is used to ask questions about distance. |
| (e) *How many miles* is it from St. Louis to Chicago? <br> (f) *How many kilometers* is it to Montreal from here? <br> (g) *How many blocks* is it to the post office? | Other ways to ask *how far:* <br>   *how many miles* <br>   *how many kilometers* <br>   *how many blocks* |

*1 mile = 1.60 kilometers.
 1 kilometer = 00.614 mile.

## 5-13 LENGTH OF TIME: *IT* + *TAKE* AND *HOW LONG*

| | |
|---|---|
| *IT* + *TAKE* + (SOMEONE) + LENGTH + INFINITIVE <br>                   OF TIME <br><br> (a) *It* takes        20 minutes *to cook* rice. <br> (b) *It* took   Al       two hours *to drive* to work. | *It* + *take* is often used with time words and an infinitive to express **length of time**, as in (a) and (b). <br> An infinitive = *to* + *the simple form of a verb.** <br> In (a): *to cook* is an infinitive. |
| (c) *How long* does it take to cook rice? —20 minutes. <br> (d) *How long* did it take Al to drive to work today? —Two hours. <br> (e) *How long* did you study last night? —Four hours. <br> (f) *How long* will you be in Hong Kong? —Ten days. | *How long* asks about **length of time**. |
| (g) *How many days* will you be in Hong Kong? | Other ways of asking *how long:* <br><br> *how many* + { *minutes* <br> *hours* <br> *days* <br> *weeks* <br> *months* <br> *years* |

*See Chart 13-3, p. 85.

## 5-14 MORE QUESTIONS WITH *HOW*

| QUESTION | ANSWER | |
|---|---|---|
| (a) *How do you spell* "coming"? <br> (b) *How do you say* "yes" in Japanese? <br> (c) *How do you say/pronounce* this word? | C-O-M-I-N-G. <br> Hai. <br> _____ | To answer (a): Spell the word. <br> To answer (b): Say the word. <br> To answer (c): Pronounce the word. |
| (d) *How are you getting along?* <br> (e) *How are you doing?* <br> (f) *How's it going?* | Great. <br> Fine. <br> Okay. <br> So-so. | In (d), (e), and (f): How is your life? Is your life okay? Do you have any problems? <br> Note: (f) is also used in greetings: *Hi, Bob. How's it going?* |
| (g) *How do you feel?* <br> *How are you feeling?* | Terrific! <br> Wonderful! <br> Great! <br> Fine. <br> Okay. <br> So-so. <br> A bit under the weather. <br> Not so good. <br> Terrible!/Lousy./Awful! | The questions in (g) ask about health or about general emotional state. |
| (h) *How do you do?* | How do you do? | *How do you do?* is used by both speakers when they are introduced to each other in a somewhat formal situation.★ |

★A: *Dr. Erickson, I'd like to introduce you to a friend of mine, Rick Brown. Rick, this is my biology professor, Dr. Erickson.*
  B: *How do you do, Mr. Brown?*
  C: *How do you do, Dr. Erickson? I'm pleased to meet you.*

## 5-15 USING *HOW ABOUT* AND *WHAT ABOUT*

| | |
|---|---|
| (a) A: We need one more player. <br> B: *How about (what about) Jack?* Let's ask him if he wants to play. <br> (b) A: What time should we meet? <br> B: *How about (what about) three o'clock?* | *How about* and *what about* have the same meaning and usage. They are used to make suggestions or offers. <br> *How about* and *what about* are followed by a noun (or pronoun) or the *-ing* form of a verb. |
| (c) A: What should we do this afternoon? <br> B: *How about going* to the zoo? <br> (d) A: *What about asking* Sally over for dinner next Sunday? <br> B: Okay. Good idea. | Note: *How about* and *what about* are frequently used in informal spoken English, but are usually not used in writing. |
| (e) A: I'm tired. *How about you?* <br> B: Yes, I'm tired too. <br> (f) A: Are you hungry? <br> B: No. *What about you?* <br> A: I'm a little hungry. | *How about you?* and *What about you?* are used to ask a question that refers to the information or question that immediately preceded it. In (e): *How about you?* = Are you tired? In (f): *What about you?* = Are you hungry? |

## 5-16 TAG QUESTIONS

| | AFFIRMATIVE (+) | NEGATIVE (−) | A tag question is a question that is added onto the end of a sentence. An auxiliary verb is used in a tag question. |
|---|---|---|---|
| (a) | *You **know** Bob Wilson,* | ***don't** you?* | |
| (b) | *Marie **is** from Paris,* | ***isn't** she?* | When the main verb is affirmative, the tag question is negative. |
| (c) | *Jerry **can play** the piano,* | ***can't** he?* | |
| | NEGATIVE (−) | AFFIRMATIVE (+) | When the main verb is negative, the tag question is affirmative. |
| (d) | *You **don't know** Jack Smith,* | ***do** you?* | |
| (e) | *Marie **isn't** from Athens,* | ***is** she?* | |
| (f) | *Jerry **can't speak** Arabic,* | ***can** he?* | |

In using a tag question, a speaker gives his idea while asking a question at the same time. In (g) and (h) below: I (the speaker) use a tag question because I expect you (the listener) to tell me that my information or my idea is correct.

As with other kinds of questions, a speaker usually uses a rising intonation at the end of a tag question.★

| | THE SPEAKER'S IDEA | THE SPEAKER'S QUESTION | EXPECTED ANSWER |
|---|---|---|---|
| (g) | I think that you know Bob Wilson. | You **know** Bob Wilson, **don't** you? | **Yes**, I do. |
| (h) | I think that you don't know Jack Smith. | You **don't know** Jack Smith, **do** you? | **No**, I **don't**. |

| COMPARE | |
|---|---|
| (i) A: Do you know Tom Lee? *(a yes/no question)* <br> B: Yes, I do. OR No, I don't. | In (i): The speaker has no idea. The speaker is simply looking for information. |
| (j) A: You know Tom Lee, don't you? *(a tag question)* <br> B: Yes, I do. | In (j): The speaker believes that the listener knows Tom Lee. The speaker wants to make sure that his idea is correct. |

★Sometimes a falling intonation is used with tag questions. For example:
   A: It's a beautiful day today, *isn't it?* *(voice falling rather than rising)*
   B: Yes, indeed. The weather's perfect.
A speaker uses falling intonation for a tag question when he is making an observation, commenting on something rather than making sure his information is correct. In the example, the speaker is making a comment about the weather to invite conversation.
   Other examples: *That was a good movie, wasn't it? Mr. Smith is a good teacher, isn't he? It's really hot today, isn't it?*

The average lifespan of a horse is more than 40 years, ***isn't it?***

ONLY 40? YOU'RE JUST A YOUNGSTER.

And sea turtles can live to be more than 200, ***can't they?***

# CHAPTER 6
## Nouns and Pronouns

---

### CONTENTS

---

## 6-1  PRONUNCIATION OF FINAL *-S/-ES*

Final *-s/-es* has three different pronunciations: /s/, /z/, and /əz/.

| | | |
|---|---|---|
| (a) | seats = seat/s/<br>maps = map/s/<br>lakes = lake/s/ | /s/ is the sound of "s" in "bus." Final *-s* is pronounced /s/ after voiceless sounds. Examples of voiceless★ sounds: /t/, /p/, /k/. |
| (b) | seeds = seed/z/<br>stars = star/z/<br>holes = hole/z/<br>laws = law/z/ | /z/ is the sound of "z" in "buzz." Final *-s* is pronounced /z/ after voiced sounds. Examples of voiced★ sounds: /d/, /r/, /l/, /m/, /b/, and all vowel sounds. |
| (c) | dishes = dish/əz/<br>matches = match/əz/<br>classes = class/əz/<br>sizes = size/əz/<br>pages = page/əz/<br>judges = judge/əz/ | /əz/ adds a whole syllable to a word. Final *-s/-es* is pronounced /əz/ after *-sh, -ch, -s, -z, -ge/-dge* sounds. |

★See Chart 2-4, p. 7, for more information about voiceless and voiced sounds.

## 6-2 PLURAL FORMS OF NOUNS

| | SINGULAR | PLURAL | |
|---|---|---|---|
| | | | To make most nouns plural, add **-s**. |
| (a) | one bird<br>one street<br>one rose | two **birds**<br>two **streets**<br>two **roses** | |
| (b) | one dish<br>one match<br>one class<br>one box | two **dishes**<br>two **matches**<br>two **classes**<br>two **boxes** | Add **-es** to nouns ending in **-sh**, **-ch**, **-ss**, and **-x**. |
| (c) | one baby<br>one city | two **babies**<br>two **cities** | If a noun ends in a consonant + **-y**, change the **y** to **i** and add **-es**, as in (c). |
| (d) | one toy<br>one key | two **toys**<br>two **keys** | If **-y** is preceded by a vowel, add only **-s**, as in (d). |
| (e) | one knife<br>one shelf | two **knives**<br>two **shelves** | If a noun ends in **-fe** or **-f**, change the ending to **-ves**. (Exceptions: *beliefs, chiefs, roofs, cuffs, cliffs*.) |
| (f) | one tomato<br>one zoo<br>one zero | two **tomatoes**<br>two **zoos**<br>two **zeroes/zeros** | The plural form of nouns that end in **-o** is sometimes **-oes** and sometimes **-os**.<br>　**-oes**: *tomatoes, potatoes, heroes, echoes*<br>　**-os**: *zoos, radios, studios, pianos, solos, sopranos, photos, autos, videos*<br>　**-oes** or **-os**: *zeroes/zeros; volcanoes/volcanos, tornadoes/tornados, mosquitoes/mosquitos* |
| (g) | one child<br>one foot<br>one goose<br>one man<br>one mouse<br>one tooth<br>one woman<br>———— | two **children**<br>two **feet**<br>two **geese**<br>two **men**<br>two **mice**<br>two **teeth**<br>two **women**<br>two **people** | Some nouns have irregular plural forms.<br>(Note: The singular form of *people* can be *person, woman, man, child*. For example, one man and one child = two people.) |
| (h) | one deer<br>one fish<br>one sheep<br>one offspring<br>one species | two **deer**<br>two **fish**<br>two **sheep**<br>two **offspring**<br>two **species** | The plural form of some nouns is the same as the singular form. |
| (i) | one bacterium<br>one cactus<br>one crisis<br>one phenomenon | two **bacteria**<br>two **cacti**<br>two **crises**<br>two **phenomena** | Some nouns that English has borrowed from other languages have foreign plurals. |

## 6-3 SUBJECTS, VERBS, AND OBJECTS

| | |
|---|---|
| (a) The **_sun_** **_shines._**<br>S V<br>(noun) (verb) <br><br>(b) **_Plants_** **_grow._**<br>S V<br>(noun) (verb) | An English sentence has a SUBJECT (**S**) and a VERB (**V**).<br><br>The SUBJECT is a **noun**. In (a): _sun_ is a noun; it is the subject of the verb _shines_. |
| (c) **_Plants_** **_need_** **_water._**<br>S V O<br>(noun) (verb) (noun)<br><br>(d) **_Bob_** **_is reading_** a **_book._**<br>S V O<br>(noun) (verb) (noun) | Sometimes a VERB is followed by an OBJECT (**O**).<br><br>The OBJECT of a verb is a **noun**. In (c): _water_ is the object of the verb _need_. |

## 6-4 OBJECTS OF PREPOSITIONS

| | |
|---|---|
| (a) Ann put her books **_on_** _the_ **_desk_**.<br>S V O PREP O OF PREP<br>(noun)<br><br>(b) A leaf fell **_to_** _the_ **_ground_**.<br>S V PREP O OF PREP<br>(noun) | Many English sentences have prepositional phrases. In (a): _on the desk_ is a prepositional phrase. A prepositional phrase consists of a PREPOSITION (**PREP**) and an OBJECT OF A PREPOSITION (**O OF PREP**). The object of a preposition is a NOUN. |

**REFERENCE LIST OF PREPOSITIONS**

| | | | | |
|---|---|---|---|---|
| _about_ | _before_ | _despite_ | _of_ | _to_ |
| _above_ | _behind_ | _down_ | _off_ | _toward(s)_ |
| _across_ | _below_ | _during_ | _on_ | _under_ |
| _after_ | _beneath_ | _for_ | _out_ | _until_ |
| _against_ | _beside_ | _from_ | _over_ | _up_ |
| _along_ | _besides_ | _in_ | _since_ | _upon_ |
| _among_ | _between_ | _into_ | _through_ | _with_ |
| _around_ | _beyond_ | _like_ | _throughout_ | _within_ |
| _at_ | _by_ | _near_ | _till_ | _without_ |

## 6-5  PREPOSITIONS OF TIME

| IN | (a) Please be on time *in the future*.<br>(b) I usually watch TV *in the evening*.<br><br>(c) I was born *in October*.<br>(d) I was born *in 1985*.<br>(e) I was born *in the twentieth century*.<br>(f) The weather is hot *in (the) summer*. | *in* + *the past, the present, the future*★<br>*in* + *the morning, the afternoon, the evening*<br><br>*in* + { a month<br>a year<br>a century<br>a season |
|---|---|---|
| ON | (g) I was born *on October 31, 1985*.<br>(h) I went to a movie *on Thursday*.<br>(i) I have class *on Thursday morning(s)*. | *on* + a date<br>*on* + a weekday<br>*on* + a weekday morning(s), afternoon(s), evening(s) |
| AT | (j) We sleep at night. I was asleep *at midnight*.<br>(k) I fell asleep *at 9:30 (nine-thirty)*.<br>(l) He's busy *at present*. Please call again. | *at* + *noon, night, midnight*<br>*at* + "*clock time*"<br>*at* + *present, the moment, the present time* |

★Possible in British English: *in future (Please be on time in future.)*.

## 6-6  WORD ORDER: PLACE AND TIME

| | |
|---|---|
|     **S**    **V**    **PLACE**    **TIME**<br>(a) Ann moved *to Paris*  *in 1998*.<br>    We went *to a movie yesterday*. | In a typical English sentence, "place" comes before "time," as in (a).<br>*INCORRECT: Ann moved in 1998 to Paris.* |
|     **S**    **V**    **O**    **P**    **T**<br>(b) We bought a house in Miami in 1995. | S-V-O-P-T = Subject-Verb-Object-Place-Time<br>S-V-O-P-T = a basic English sentence structure. |
|     **TIME**    **S**    **V**    **PLACE**<br>(c) *In 1998,* Ann moved to Paris.<br>(d) *Yesterday* we went to a movie. | Expressions of time can also come at the beginning of a sentence, as in (c) and (d). A time phrase at the beginning of a sentence is often followed by a comma, as in (c). |

    **S**    **V**    **O**    **P**    **T**
Anna bought some cheese at the deli yesterday.

## 6-7 SUBJECT–VERB AGREEMENT

| | |
|---|---|
| SINGULAR  SINGULAR<br>(a) The sun  shine**s**.<br><br>PLURAL  PLURAL<br>(b) *Birds*  *sing.* | A singular subject takes a singular verb, as in (a).<br>A plural subject takes a plural verb, as in (b).<br><br>Notice: *verb* + **-s** = singular (*shines*)<br>  *noun* + **-s** = plural (*birds*) |
| SINGULAR  SINGULAR<br>(c) *My brother*  **lives**  in Jakarta.<br><br>  PLURAL  PLURAL<br>(d) *My brother **and** sister*  **live**  in Jakarta. | Two subjects connected by ***and*** take a plural verb, as in (d). |
| (e) The ***glasses*** over there under the window by the sink ***are*** clean.<br>(f) The ***information*** in those magazines about Vietnamese culture and customs ***is*** very interesting. | Sometimes phrases come between a subject and a verb. These phrases do not affect the agreement of the subject and verb. |
| v  s<br>(g) *There **is** a **book** on the desk.*<br><br>v  s<br>(h) *There **are** some **books** on the desk.* | ***There*** + ***be*** + *subject* expresses that something exists in a particular place. The verb agrees with the noun that follows ***be***. |
| (i) ***Every student is*** sitting down.<br>(j) ***Everybody/Everyone hopes*** for peace. | ***Every*** is a singular word. It is used with a singular, not plural, noun.<br>*INCORRECT: Every students . . . .*<br>Subjects with ***every*** take singular verbs, as in (i) and (j). |
| (k) ***People*** in my country ***are*** friendly. | ***People*** is a plural noun and takes a plural verb. |

There ***are*** four little ***birds*** in the nest.

## 6-8  USING ADJECTIVES TO DESCRIBE NOUNS

| | |
|---|---|
|                **ADJ  NOUN**<br>(a) Bob is reading a **good** book. | Words that describe nouns are called *adjectives*.<br>In (a): **good** is an adjective; it describes the book. |
| (b) The **tall** *woman* wore a **new** *dress*.<br>(c) The **short** *woman* wore an **old** *dress*.<br>(d) The **young** *woman* wore a **short** *dress*. | We say that adjectives "modify" nouns.  "Modify" means "change a little."  An adjective changes the meaning of a noun by giving more information about it. |
| (e) Roses are **beautiful** *flowers*.<br>     *INCORRECT: Roses are beautifuls flowers.* | Adjectives are neither singular nor plural.  They do NOT have a plural form. |
| (f) He wore a **white** shirt.<br>     *INCORRECT: He wore a shirt white.*<br>(g) Roses *are* **beautiful**.<br>(h) His shirt *was* **white**. | Adjectives usually come immediately before nouns, as in (f).<br>Adjectives can also follow main verb *be*, as in (g) and (h). |

Crocodiles have **big** teeth.

## 6-9  USING NOUNS AS ADJECTIVES

| | |
|---|---|
| (a) I have a **flower** *garden*.<br>(b) The **shoe** *store* also sells socks.<br>(c) *INCORRECT: a flowers garden*<br>(d) *INCORRECT: the shoes store* | Sometimes words that are usually used as nouns are used as adjectives.  For example, *flower* is usually a noun, but in (a) it is used as an adjective to modify *garden*.  When a noun is used as an adjective, it is singular in form, NOT plural. |

### PERSONAL PRONOUNS

| | | | | | |
|---|---|---|---|---|---|
| **SUBJECT PRONOUNS:** | *I* | *we* | *you* | *he, she, it* | *they* |
| **OBJECT PRONOUNS:** | *me* | *us* | *you* | *him, her, it* | *them* |

| | |
|---|---|
| (a) **Kate** is married. **She** has two children. <br> *S* | A pronoun refers to a noun. <br> In (a): **she** is a pronoun; it refers to **Kate**. <br> In (b): **her** is a pronoun; it refers to **Kate**. <br> **She** is a subject pronoun; **her** is an object pronoun. |
| (b) **Kate** is my friend.  I know **her** well. <br> *O* | |
| (c) Mike has **a new blue bicycle**. <br> He bought **it** yesterday. | A pronoun can refer to a single noun (e.g., *Kate*) or to a noun phrase.  In (c): **it** refers to the whole noun phrase *a new blue bicycle*. |
| (d) *Eric and **I*** are good friends. <br> *S* | Guidelines for using pronouns following **and**: <br> If the pronoun is used as part of the subject, use a subject pronoun, as in (d).  If it is part of the object, use an object pronoun, as in (e) and (f). |
| (e) Ann met *Eric and **me*** at the museum. <br> *O* | *INCORRECT: Eric and me are good friends.* <br> *INCORRECT: Ann met Eric and I at the museum.* |
| (f) Ann walked between *Eric and **me**.* <br> *O of PREP* | |

| | | | | | |
|---|---|---|---|---|---|
| **SINGULAR PRONOUNS:** | *I* | *me* | *you* | *he, she, it* | *him, her* |
| **PLURAL PRONOUNS:** | *we* | *us* | *you* | *they* | *them* |

| | |
|---|---|
| (g) **Mike** is in class.  **He** is taking a test. <br> (h) The **students** are in class.  **They** are taking a test. <br> (i) **Kate and Tom** are married.  **They** have two children. | *Singular* = one.  *Plural* = more than one.  Singular pronouns refer to singular nouns, plural pronouns to plural nouns, as in the examples. |

Adam and Amanda have a son named Jim.
***They*** are waiting for a phone call from ***him***.

## 6-11 POSSESSIVE NOUNS

| | | |
|---|---|---|
| SINGULAR: (a) I know the **student's** name.<br>PLURAL:   (b) I know the **students'** names.<br>PLURAL:   (c) I know the **children's** names. | | An apostrophe (') and an **-s** are used with nouns to show possession. |

| | | | |
|---|---|---|---|
| **Singular** | (d) the student<br>my baby<br>a man | → the **student's** name<br>→ my **baby's** name<br>→ a **man's** name | SINGULAR POSSESSIVE NOUN:<br>*noun + apostrophe (') + **-s*** |
| | (e) James | → **James'/James's** name | A singular noun that ends in *-s* has two possible possessive forms: *James'* OR *James's*. |
| **Plural** | (f) the students<br>my babies | → the **students'** names<br>→ my **babies'** names | PLURAL POSSESSIVE NOUN:<br>*noun + **-s** + apostrophe (')* |
| | (g) men<br>the children | → **men's** names<br>→ the **children's** names | IRREGULAR PLURAL POSSESSIVE NOUN:<br>*noun + apostrophe (') + **-s***<br>(An irregular plural noun is a plural noun that does not end in **-s**: *children, men, people, women.* See Chart 6-2, p. 39.) |
| | COMPARE<br>(h) **Tom's** here.<br>(i) **Tom's** brother is here. | | In (h): **Tom's** is not a possessive. It is a contraction of *Tom is*, used in informal writing.<br>In (i): **Tom's** is a possessive. |

## 6-12 POSSESSIVE PRONOUNS AND ADJECTIVES

| | |
|---|---|
| This pen belongs to me.<br>(a) It's **mine**.<br>(b) It is **my** pen. | (a) and (b) have the same meaning; they both show possession. **Mine** is a *possessive pronoun*; **my** is a *possessive adjective*. |

| POSSESSIVE PRONOUNS | POSSESSIVE ADJECTIVES | |
|---|---|---|
| (c) I have **mine**. | I have **my** pen. | A **possessive pronoun** is used alone, without a noun following it. |
| (d) You have **yours**. | You have **your** pen. | |
| (e) She has **hers**. | She has **her** pen. | A **possessive adjective** is used only with a noun following it. |
| (f) He has **his**. | He has **his** pen. | INCORRECT: *I have mine pen.* |
| (g) We have **ours**. | We have **our** pens. | INCORRECT: *I have my.* |
| (h) You have **yours**. | You have **your** pen. | |
| (i) They have **theirs**. | They have **their** pens. | |
| (j) —————— | I have a book. **Its** cover is black. | |
| COMPARE *its* vs. *it's*:<br>(k) Sue gave me a book. I don't remember **its** title.<br>(l) Sue gave me a book. **It's** a novel. | | In (k): **its** (NO apostrophe) is a possessive adjective modifying the noun *title*.<br>In (l): **It's** (with an apostrophe) is a contraction of *it + is*. |
| COMPARE *their* vs. *there* vs. *they're*:<br>(m) The students have **their** books.<br>(n) My books are over **there**.<br>(o) Where are the students? **They're** in class. | | **Their, there,** and **they're** have the same pronunciation, but not the same meaning.<br>**their** = possessive adjective, as in (m).<br>**there** = an expression of place, as in (n).<br>**they're** = *they are*, as in (o). |

| | | |
|---|---|---|
| *myself* | (a) *I saw **myself** in the mirror.* | Reflexive pronouns end in ***-self/-selves***. They are used when the subject (e.g., *I*) and the object (e.g., *myself*) are the same person. The action of the verb is pointed back to the subject of the sentence. |
| *yourself* | (b) *You* (one person) *saw **yourself**.* | |
| *herself* | (c) *She saw **herself**.* | |
| *himself* | (d) *He saw **himself**.* | |
| *itself* | (e) *It* (e.g., the kitten) *saw **itself**.* | *INCORRECT: I saw me in the mirror.* |
| *ourselves* | (f) *We saw **ourselves**.* | |
| *yourselves* | (g) *You* (plural) *saw **yourselves**.* | |
| *themselves* | (h) *They saw **themselves**.* | |

| | |
|---|---|
| (i) *Greg lives **by himself**.* | ***By** + a reflexive pronoun* = alone. In (i): Greg lives alone, without family or roommates. |
| (j) *I sat **by myself** on the park bench.* | |

| | |
|---|---|
| (k) *I **enjoyed myself** at the fair.* | *Enjoy* and a few other verbs are commonly followed by a reflexive pronoun. See the list below. |

COMMON EXPRESSIONS WITH REFLEXIVE PRONOUNS

| | | | |
|---|---|---|---|
| *believe in yourself* | *help yourself* | *pinch yourself* | *teach yourself* |
| *blame yourself* | *hurt yourself* | *be proud of yourself* | *tell yourself* |
| *cut yourself* | *give yourself (something)* | *take care of yourself* | *work for yourself* |
| *enjoy yourself* | *introduce yourself* | *talk to yourself* | *wish yourself (luck)* |
| *feel sorry for yourself* | *kill yourself* | | |

*He* saw ***himself*** in the mirror.

*She* saw ***herself*** in the mirror.

He *kitten* saw ***itself*** in the mirror.

## 6-14 SINGULAR FORMS OF *OTHER: ANOTHER* vs. *THE OTHER*

**ANOTHER**

| | |
|---|---|
| (a) There is a large bowl of apples on the table. Paul is going to eat one apple. If he is still hungry after that, he can eat **another** apple. There are many apples to choose from. | ***Another*** means "one more out of a group of similar items, one in addition to the one(s) already mentioned." <br><br> ***Another*** is a combination of *an* + *other*, written as one word. |

**THE OTHER**

| | |
|---|---|
| (b) There are two apples on the table. Paul is going to eat one of them. Sara is going to eat **the other** apple. | ***The other*** means "the last one in a specific group, the only one that remains from a given number of similar items." |

| | | |
|---|---|---|
| (c) Paul ate one apple. Then he ate | *another* apple. <br> *another* one. <br> *another*. | ***Another*** and ***the other*** can be used as adjectives in front of a noun (e.g., *apple*) or in front of the word *one*. <br><br> ***Another*** and ***the other*** can also be used alone as pronouns. |
| (d) Paul ate one apple. Sara ate | *the other* apple. <br> *the other* one. <br> *the other*. | |

**OTHER(S)**

| | |
|---|---|
| There are many apples in Paul's kitchen.  Paul is holding one apple. | **Other(s)** (without **the**) means "several more out of a group of similar items, several in addition to the one(s) already mentioned." The adjective **other** (without an **-s**) can be used with a plural noun (e.g., *apples*) or with the word *ones*. |
| (a) There are **other** *apples* in a bowl.<br>  (adjective) + (noun) | |
| (b) There are **other** *ones* on a plate.<br>  (adjective) + (ones) | **Others** (with an **-s**) is a plural pronoun; it is not used with a noun. |
| (c) There are **others** on a chair.<br>  (pronoun) | In (c): **others = other apples**. |

**THE OTHER(S)**

| | |
|---|---|
| There are four apples on the table.  Paul is going to take one of them. | **The other(s)** means "the last ones in a specific group, the remains from a given number of similar items." |
| (d) Sara is going to take **the other** *apples*.<br>  (adjective) + (noun) | **The other** (without an **-s**) can be used as an adjective in front of a noun or the word *ones*, as in (d) and (e). |
| (e) Sara is going to take **the other** *ones*.<br>  (adjective) + (ones) | **The others** (with an **-s**) is a plural pronoun; it is not used with a noun. |
| (f) Sara is going to take **the others**.<br>  (pronoun) | In (f): **the others = the other apples**. |

## 6-16   SUMMARY OF FORMS OF *OTHER*

| | **ADJECTIVE** | **PRONOUN** | |
|---|---|---|---|
| SINGULAR<br>PLURAL | another apple<br>other apples | another<br>other**s** | Notice that the word **others** (*other* + *final* **-s**) is used only as a plural pronoun. |
| SINGULAR<br>PLURAL | the other apple<br>the other apples | the other<br>the other**s** | |

# CHAPTER 7
# Modal Auxiliaries

## CONTENTS

## 7-1  THE FORM OF MODAL AUXILIARIES

The verbs listed below are called "modal auxiliaries." They are helping verbs that express a wide range of meanings (ability, permission, possibility, necessity, etc.).  Most of the modals have more than one meaning.

| AUXILIARY + THE SIMPLE FORM OF A VERB | | *Can, could, may, might, should, had better, must, will,* and *would* are immediately followed by the simple form of a verb. |
|---|---|---|
| can | (a) Olga **can speak** English. | • They are not followed by **to**.<br>     *INCORRECT: Olga can to speak English.* |
| could | (b) He **couldn't come** to class. | • The main verb does not have a final **-s**.<br>     *INCORRECT: Olga can speaks English.* |
| may | (c) It **may rain** tomorrow. | |
| might | (d) It **might rain** tomorrow. | • The main verb is not in a past form.<br>     *INCORRECT: Olga can spoke English.* |
| should | (e) Mary **should study** harder. | |
| had better | (f) I **had better study** tonight. | • The main verb is not in its **-ing** form.<br>     *INCORRECT: Olga can speaking English.* |
| must | (g) Joe **must see** a doctor today. | |
| will | (h) I **will be** in class tomorrow. | |
| would | (i) **Would** you please **close** the door? | |
| AUXILIARY + **TO** + THE SIMPLE FORM OF A VERB | | **To** + *the simple form* is used with these auxiliaries: *have to, have got to,* and *ought to*. |
| have to | (j) I **have to study** tonight. | |
| have got to | (k) I **have got to study** tonight. | |
| ought to | (l) Kate **ought to study** harder. | |

## 7-2 EXPRESSING ABILITY: *CAN* AND *COULD*

| | |
|---|---|
| (a) Bob *can play* the piano.<br>(b) You *can buy* a screwdriver at a hardware store.<br>(c) I *can meet* you at Ted's tomorrow afternoon. | *Can* expresses *ability* in the present or future. |
| (d) I $\begin{Bmatrix} can't \\ cannot \\ can\ not \end{Bmatrix}$ understand that sentence. | The negative form of *can* may be written *can't*, *cannot*, or *can not*. |
| (e) Our son *could walk* when he was one year old. | The past form of *can* is *could*. |
| (f) He *couldn't walk* when he was six months old. | The negative of *could*: *couldn't* or *could not*. |

## 7-3 EXPRESSING POSSIBILITY: *MAY* AND *MIGHT*<br>EXPRESSING PERMISSION: *MAY* AND *CAN*

| | |
|---|---|
| (a) It *may rain* tomorrow.<br>(b) It *might rain* tomorrow.<br>(c) A: Why isn't John in class?<br>    B: I don't know. He $\begin{Bmatrix} may \\ might \end{Bmatrix}$ be sick today. | *May* and *might* express *possibility* in the present or future. They have the same meaning. There is no difference in meaning between (a) and (b). |
| (d) It *may not rain* tomorrow.<br>(e) It *might not rain* tomorrow. | Negative: *may not* and *might not*. (Do not contract *may* and *might* with *not*.) |
| (f) *Maybe* it will rain tomorrow.<br>COMPARE<br>(g) *Maybe* John is sick. *(adverb)*<br>(h) John *may be* sick. *(verb)* | In (f) and (g): *maybe* (spelled as one word) is an adverb. It means "possibly." It comes at the beginning of a sentence.<br>    *INCORRECT: It will maybe rain tomorrow.*<br>In (h): *may be* (two words) is a verb form: the auxiliary *may* + *the main verb* *be*.<br>    *INCORRECT: John maybe sick.* |
| (i) Yes, children, you *may have* a cookie after dinner.<br>(j) Okay, kids, you *can have* a cookie after dinner. | *May* is also used to give *permission*, as in (i).<br>Often *can* is used to give *permission*, too, as in (j).<br>(i) and (j) have the same meaning, but *may* is more formal than *can*. |
| (k) You *may not have* a cookie.<br>    You *can't have* a cookie. | *May not* and *cannot* (*can't*) are used to deny permission (i.e., to say "no"). |

## 7-4 USING *COULD* TO EXPRESS POSSIBILITY

| | |
|---|---|
| (a) A: Why isn't Greg in class?<br>   B: I don't know. He *could be* sick.<br><br>(b) Look at those dark clouds. It *could start* raining any minute. | ***Could*** can mean *past ability*. (See Chart 7-2, p. 50.) But that is not its only meaning. Another meaning of ***could*** is *possibility*.<br><br>In (a): "He *could* be sick" has the same meaning as "He *may/might* be sick," i.e., "It is possible that he is sick."<br><br>In (a): ***could*** expresses a **present** possibility.<br>In (b): ***could*** expresses a **future** possibility. |

## 7-5 POLITE QUESTIONS: *MAY I, COULD I, CAN I*

| POLITE QUESTION | POSSIBLE ANSWERS | |
|---|---|---|
| (a) *May I* please borrow your pen?<br>(b) *Could I* please borrow your pen?<br>(c) *Can I* please borrow your pen? | Yes.<br>Yes. Of course.<br>Yes. Certainly.<br>Of course.<br>Certainly.<br>Sure. (informal)<br>Okay. (informal)<br>Uh-huh. (meaning "yes")<br>I'm sorry, but I need to<br>   use it myself. | People use *may I, could I,*★ and *can I* to ask polite questions. The questions ask for someone's permission or agreement. (a), (b), and (c) have basically the same meaning.<br>Note: *can I* is less formal than *may I* and *could I*.<br><br>*Please* can come at the end of the question: *May I borrow your pen, please?*<br><br>*Please* can be omitted from the question: *May I borrow your pen?* |

★In a polite question, *could* is NOT the past form of *can*.

## 7-6 POLITE QUESTIONS: *WOULD YOU, COULD YOU, WILL YOU, CAN YOU*

| POLITE QUESTION | POSSIBLE ANSWERS | |
|---|---|---|
| (a) *Would you* please open the door?<br>(b) *Could you* please open the door?<br>(c) *Will you* please open the door?<br>(d) *Can you* please open the door? | Yes.<br>Yes. Of course.<br>Certainly. I'd be happy to.<br>Of course. I'd be glad to.<br>Sure. (informal)<br>Okay. (informal)<br>Uh-huh. (meaning "yes")<br>I'm sorry. I'd like to help,<br>   but my hands are full. | People use *would you, could you, will you*, and *can you* to ask polite questions. The questions ask for someone's help or cooperation. (a), (b), (c), and (d) have basically the same meaning. The use of *can*, as in (d), is less formal than the others.<br><br>Note: *May* is NOT used when *you* is the subject of a polite question.<br>*INCORRECT: May you please open the door?* |

## 7-7 EXPRESSING ADVICE: *SHOULD* AND *OUGHT TO*

| | |
|---|---|
| (a) My clothes are dirty I $\left\{ \begin{array}{l} \textbf{\textit{should}} \\ \textbf{\textit{ought to}} \end{array} \right\}$ wash them. <br><br> (b) INCORRECT: *I should to wash them.* <br> (c) INCORRECT: *I ought washing them.* | **Should** and **ought to** have the same meaning. They mean: "This is a good idea. This is good advice." <br><br> FORMS: <br>     *should* + simple form of a verb (no *to*) <br>     *ought* + *to* + simple form of a verb |
| (d) You need your sleep. You **should not** (**shouldn't**) stay up late. | NEGATIVE: *should* + *not* = *shouldn't* <br> (*Ought to* is usually not used in the negative.) |
| (e) A: I'm going to be late. What **should I do?** <br>     B: Run. | QUESTION: *should* + subject + main verb <br> (*Ought to* is usually not used in questions.) |
| (f) A: I'm tired today. <br>     B: You *should/ought to* go home and take a nap. <br><br> (g) A: I'm tired today. <br>     B: **Maybe** you *should/ought to* go home and take a nap. | The use of **maybe** with **should** and **ought to** "softens" advice. COMPARE: <br><br> In (f): Speaker B is giving definite advice. He is stating clearly that he believes going home for a nap is a good idea and is the solution to Speaker A's problem. <br><br> In (g): Speaker B is making a suggestion: going home for a nap is one possible way to solve Speaker A's problem. |

## 7-8 EXPRESSING ADVICE: *HAD BETTER*

| | |
|---|---|
| (a) My clothes are dirty. I $\left\{ \begin{array}{l} \textbf{\textit{should}} \\ \textbf{\textit{ought to}} \\ \textbf{\textit{had better}} \end{array} \right\}$ *wash* them. <br><br> (b) You're driving too fast! You**'d better** *slow* down. | **Had better** has the same basic meaning as *should* and *ought to:* "This is a good idea. This is good advice." |
| | **Had better** usually implies a warning about possible bad consequences. In (b): If you don't slow down, there could be a bad result. You could get a speeding ticket or have an accident. |
| (c) You**'d better not** *eat* that meat. It looks spoiled. | NEGATIVE: *had better not* |
| (d) **I'd** *better send* my boss an e-mail right away. | In speaking, **had** is usually contracted: *'d.* |

Ted **had better** *change* his clothes
before he goes to his job interview.

## 7-9 EXPRESSING NECESSITY: *HAVE TO, HAVE GOT TO, MUST*

| | |
|---|---|
| (a) I have a very important test tomorrow.<br><br>I { *have to*<br>*have got to*<br>*must* } *study* tonight. | ***Have to***, ***have got to***, and ***must*** have basically the same meaning. They express the idea that something is *necessary*. |
| (b) I'd like to go with you to the movie this evening, but I can't. I ***have to go*** to a meeting.<br>(c) Bye now! I***'ve got to go***. My wife's waiting for me. I'll call you later.<br>(d) All passengers ***must present*** their passports at customs upon arrival. | ***Have to*** is used much more frequently in everyday speech and writing than ***must***.<br><br>***Have got to*** is typically used in informal conversation, as in (c).<br>***Must*** is typically found in written instructions, as in (d). It is usually a strong, serious, "no nonsense" word. |
| (e) ***Do*** we ***have to bring*** pencils to the test?<br>(f) Why ***did*** he ***have to leave*** so early? | QUESTIONS: ***Have to*** is usually used in questions, not ***must*** or ***have got to***. Forms of ***do*** are used with ***have to*** in questions. |
| (g) I ***had to*** *study* last night. | The PAST form of ***have to***, ***have got to***, and ***must*** (meaning necessity) is ***had to***. |
| (h) I ***have to*** ("hafta") *go* downtown today.<br>(i) Rita ***has to*** ("hasta") *go* to the bank.<br>(j) I've ***got to*** ("gotta") *study* tonight. | Usual PRONUNCIATION:<br>    ***have to*** = /hæftə/ OR /hæftu/<br>    ***has to*** = /hæstə/ OR /hæstu/<br>    *(have)* ***got to*** = /gadə/ OR /gɔtə/ |

## 7-10 EXPRESSING LACK OF NECESSITY: *DO NOT HAVE TO*<br>EXPRESSING PROHIBITION: *MUST NOT*

| | |
|---|---|
| (a) I finished all of my homework this afternoon. I ***don't have to study*** tonight.<br>(b) Tomorrow is a holiday. Mary ***doesn't have to go*** to class. | ***Don't/doesn't have to*** expresses the idea that something is *not necessary*. |
| (c) Children, you ***must not play*** with matches!<br>(d) We ***must not use*** that door. The sign says PRIVATE: DO NOT ENTER. | ***Must not*** expresses *prohibition* (DO NOT DO THIS!). |
| (e) You ***mustn't play*** with matches. | ***Must*** + ***not*** = ***mustn't***. (Note: The first "t" is not pronounced.) |

## 7-11  MAKING LOGICAL CONCLUSIONS: *MUST*

| | |
|---|---|
| (a) A: Nancy is yawning.<br>   B: She ***must be*** sleepy. | In (a): Speaker B is making a logical guess. He bases his guess on the information that Nancy is yawning. His logical conclusion, his "best guess," is that Nancy is sleepy. He uses ***must*** to express his logical conclusion. |
| (b) LOGICAL CONCLUSION: Amy plays tennis every day. She ***must like*** to play tennis.<br>(c) NECESSITY: If you want to get into the movie theater, you ***must buy*** a ticket. | COMPARE: ***Must*** can express<br> • a logical conclusion, as in (b).<br> • necessity, as in (c). |
| (d) NEGATIVE LOGICAL CONCLUSION: Eric ate everything on his plate except the pickle. He ***must not like*** pickles.<br>(e) PROHIBITION: There are sharks in the ocean near our hotel. We ***must not go*** swimming there. | COMPARE: ***Must not*** can express<br> • a negative logical conclusion, as in (d).<br> • prohibition, as in (e). |

## 7-12  GIVING INSTRUCTIONS: IMPERATIVE SENTENCES

| | |
|---|---|
| COMMAND<br>(a) *General:*  ***Open*** the door!<br>   *Soldier:*  Yes, sir!<br><br>REQUEST<br>(b) *Teacher:*  ***Open*** the door, please.<br>   *Student:*  Okay, I'd be happy to.<br><br>DIRECTIONS<br>(c) *Barbara:*  Could you tell me how to get to the post office?<br>   *Stranger:*  Certainly. ***Walk*** two blocks down this street. ***Turn*** left and ***walk*** three more blocks. It's on the right-hand side of the street. | Imperative sentences are used to give commands, make polite requests, and give directions. The difference between a command and a request lies in the speaker's tone of voice and the use of ***please***.<br>***Please*** can come at the beginning or end of a request:<br>   *Open the door, please.*<br>   *Please open the door.* |
| (d) ***Close*** the window.<br>(e) Please ***sit*** down.<br>(f) ***Be*** quiet!<br>(g) ***Don't walk*** on the grass.<br>(h) Please ***don't wait*** for me.<br>(i) ***Don't be*** late. | The simple form of a verb is used in imperative sentences. The understood subject of the sentence is ***you*** (meaning the person the speaker is talking to): *(You) close the window.*<br>NEGATIVE FORM:<br>   ***Don't*** + *the simple form of a verb* |

## 7-13 MAKING SUGGESTIONS: *LET'S* AND *WHY DON'T*

| | |
|---|---|
| (a) A: It's hot today. ***Let's go*** to the beach.<br>B: Okay. Good idea.<br>(b) A: It's hot today. ***Why don't we go*** to the beach?<br>B: Okay. Good idea. | ***Let's*** (do something) and ***why don't we*** (do something) have the same meaning. They are used to make suggestions about activities for you and me. ***Let's*** = let us. |
| (c) A: I'm tired.<br>B: ***Why don't you take*** a nap?<br>A: That's a good idea. I think I will. | ***Why don't you*** (do something) is used to make a friendly suggestion, to give friendly advice. |

## 7-14 STATING PREFERENCES: *PREFER, LIKE ... BETTER, WOULD RATHER*

| | |
|---|---|
| (a) I ***prefer*** apples ***to*** oranges.<br>(b) I ***prefer*** watching TV ***to*** *studying*. | ***prefer*** + noun + ***to*** + noun<br>***prefer*** + -ing verb + ***to*** + -ing verb |
| (c) I ***like*** apples ***better than*** oranges.<br>(d) I ***like*** watching TV ***better than*** studying. | ***like*** + noun + ***better than*** + noun<br>***like*** + -ing verb + ***better than*** + -ing verb |
| (e) Ann ***would rather have*** an apple than an orange.<br>(f) *INCORRECT: Ann would rather has an apple.*<br>(g) I'd rather visit a big city ***than live*** there.<br>(h) *INCORRECT: I'd rather visit a big city than to live there.*<br>*INCORRECT: I'd rather visit a big city than living there.* | ***Would rather*** is followed immediately by the simple form of a verb (e.g., *have, visit, live*).<br><br>Verbs following ***than*** are also in the simple form. |
| (i) ***I'd/You'd/She'd/He'd/We'd/They'd*** rather have an apple. | Contraction of ***would*** = ***'d***. |
| (j) ***Would you rather*** have an apple ***or*** an orange? | In (j): In a polite question, ***would rather*** can be followed by ***or*** to offer someone a choice. |

A cat ***would rather*** be in a warm, dry place than outside during a rainstorm.

A duck ***prefers*** *swimming* in water *to being* in a warm, dry place.

# CHAPTER 8
## Connecting Ideas

### CONTENTS

## 8-1   CONNECTING IDEAS WITH *AND*

| | |
|---|---|
| **CONNECTING ITEMS WITHIN A SENTENCE** <br><br> (a) NO COMMA:  I saw a cat *and* a mouse. <br> (b) COMMAS:    I saw a cat**,** a mouse**,** *and* a dog. | When *and* connects only **two** words (or phrases) within a sentence, NO COMMA is used, as in (a). <br> When *and* connects **three or more** items within a sentence, COMMAS are used, as in (b).★ |
| **CONNECTING TWO SENTENCES** <br><br> (c) COMMA:      I saw a cat**,** *and* you saw a mouse. | When *and* connects two complete sentences (also called independent clauses), a comma is usually used, as in (c). |
| (d) PERIOD:       I saw a cat**.** You saw a mouse. <br> (e) *INCORRECT: I saw a cat, you saw a mouse.* | Without ***and***, two complete sentences are separated by a period, as in (d), NOT a comma.★★ A complete sentence begins with a capital letter; note that *You* is capitalized in (d). |

★In a series of three or more items, the comma before *and* is optional.

ALSO CORRECT: *I saw a cat**,** a mouse and a dog.*

★★A "period" (the dot used at the end of a sentence) is called a "full stop" in British English.

## 8-2 CONNECTING IDEAS WITH *BUT* AND *OR*

| | |
|---|---|
| (a) I *went* to bed **but** *couldn't sleep.*<br>(b) Is a lemon *sweet* **or** *sour?*<br>(c) Did you order *coffee*, *tea*, **or** *milk?* | ***And, but,*** and ***or*** are called "conjunctions."*<br>Like ***and, but*** and ***or*** can connect items within a sentence.<br>Commas are used with a series of three or more items, as in (c). |
| *I dropped the vase.* = a sentence<br>*It didn't break.* = a sentence<br>(d) I dropped the vase, **but** it didn't break.<br>(e) Do we have class on Monday, **or** is Monday a holiday? | A comma is usually used when ***but*** or ***or*** combines two complete (independent) sentences into one sentence, as in (d) and (e).** |

*More specifically, *and*, *but*, and *or* are called "coordinating conjunctions."

**Except in very formal writing, a conjunction can also come at the beginning of a sentence.

ALSO CORRECT: *I dropped the vase.* ***B****ut it didn't break.*

*I saw a cat.* ***A****nd you saw a mouse.*

## 8-3 CONNECTING IDEAS WITH *SO*

| | |
|---|---|
| (a) The room was dark, **so** I turned on a light. | ***So*** can be used as a conjunction. It is preceded by a comma. It connects the ideas in two independent clauses. ***So*** expresses **results**:<br>cause: *The room was dark.*<br>result: *I turned on a light.* |
| (b) COMPARE: The room was dark, **but** I didn't turn on a light. | ***But*** often expresses an unexpected result, as in (b). |

## 8-4 USING AUXILIARY VERBS AFTER *BUT* AND *AND*

| | |
|---|---|
| (a) I ***don't like*** coffee, **but** my husband ***does.***<br>(b) I ***like*** tea, **but** my husband ***doesn't.***<br>(c) I ***won't be*** here tomorrow, **but** Sue ***will.***<br>(d) I***'ve seen*** that movie, **but** Joe ***hasn't.***<br>(e) He ***isn't*** here, **but** she ***is.**** | In (a): ***does*** = *likes coffee.* After ***but*** and ***and***, often only an auxiliary verb is used. It has the same tense or modal as the main verb. |
| (f) I ***don't like*** coffee, **and** Ed ***doesn't*** either.<br>(g) I ***like*** tea, **and** Kate ***does*** too.<br>(h) I ***won't be*** here, **and** he ***won't*** either.<br>(i) I***'ve seen*** that movie, **and** Pat ***has*** too.<br>(j) He ***isn't*** here, **and** Anna ***isn't*** either. | Notice in the examples:<br>negative + *but* + affirmative<br>affirmative + *but* + negative<br><br>negative + *and* + negative<br>affirmative + *and* + affirmative |

*A verb is not contracted with a pronoun at the end of a sentence after *but* and *and:*

CORRECT: . . . *but she is.*

INCORRECT: . . . *but she's.*

## 8-5 USING *AND* + *TOO, SO, EITHER, NEITHER*

| | |
|---|---|
| (a) Sue works, *and* **Tom** **does** **too.**<br><center>S + aux + TOO</center><br>(b) Sue works, *and* **so** **does** **Tom.**<br><center>SO + aux + S</center> | (a) and (b) have the same meaning.<br>Word order:<br>    *subject* + *auxiliary* + **too**<br>    **so** + *auxiliary* + *subject* |
| (c) Ann doesn't work, *and* **Joe** **doesn't** **either.**<br><center>S + aux + EITHER</center><br>(d) Ann doesn't work, *and* **neither** **does** **Joe.**<br><center>NEITHER + aux + S</center> | (c) and (d) have the same meaning.<br>Word order:<br>    *subject* + *auxiliary* + **either**<br>    **neither** + *auxiliary* + *subject*<br>Note: An affirmative auxiliary is used with *neither.* |
| (e) A: I'm hungry.<br>    B: ***I am too.***      (f) A: I'm hungry.<br>                      B: ***So am I.***<br>(g) A: I don't eat meat.   (h) A: I don't eat meat.<br>    B: ***I don't either.***             B: ***Neither do I.*** | ***And*** is usually not used when there are two speakers.<br>(e) and (f) have the same meaning.<br>(g) and (h) have the same meaning. |
| (i) A: I'm hungry.         (j) A: I don't eat meat.<br>    B: ***Me too.*** (informal)     B: ***Me neither.*** (informal) | ***Me too*** and ***me neither*** are often used in informal spoken English. |

James has a mustache,
*and* **so does Marco**.

James

Ivan

Ivan isn't wearing a hat,
*and James isn't* **either**.

Omar doesn't have a mustache,
*and* **neither does Ivan**.

Omar

Marco

Marco has a mustache,
*and* **James does too**.

## 8-6 CONNECTING IDEAS WITH *BECAUSE*

| | |
|---|---|
| (a) He drank water *because* he was thirsty. | ***Because*** expresses a cause; it gives a reason. Why did he drink water?  Reason: he was thirsty. |
| (b) MAIN CLAUSE: *He drank water.* | A main clause is a complete sentence:<br>*He drank water* = a complete sentence. |
| (c) ADVERB CLAUSE: *because he was thirsty* | An adverb clause is NOT a complete sentence:<br>*because he was thirsty* = NOT a complete sentence.<br>***Because*** introduces an adverb clause:<br>***because*** + *subject* + *verb* = *an adverb clause.* |
| MAIN CLAUSE ADVERB CLAUSE<br>(d) He drank water *because he was thirsty.*<br>(no comma)<br><br>ADVERB CLAUSE MAIN CLAUSE<br>(e) *Because he was thirsty,* he drank water.<br>(comma) | An adverb clause is connected to a main clause, as in (d) and (e).★<br>In (d): **main clause** + ***no* comma** + **adverb clause**<br>In (e): **adverb clause** + **comma** + **main clause**<br><br>(d) and (e) have exactly the same meaning. |
| (f) *INCORRECT IN WRITING:*<br>*He drank water.* **Because he was thirsty.** | (f) is incorrect in written English: *because he was thirsty* cannot stand alone as a sentence that starts with a capital letter and ends with a period.  It has to be connected to a main clause, as in (d) and (e). |
| (g) CORRECT IN SPEAKING:<br>A:  Why did he drink some water?<br>B:  **Because he was thirsty.** | In spoken English, an adverb clause can be used as the short answer to a question, as in (g). |

★See Chart 2-10, p. 12, for a discussion of other adverb clauses.  "Time clauses" are adverb clauses that are introduced by *when, after, before, while, until,* and *as soon as.*

## 8-7 CONNECTING IDEAS WITH *EVEN THOUGH / ALTHOUGH*

| | |
|---|---|
| (a) ***Even though*** *I was hungry,* I did not eat.<br>I did not eat ***even though*** *I was hungry.*<br>(b) ***Although*** *I was hungry,* I did not eat.<br>I did not eat ***although*** *I was hungry.* | ***Even though*** and ***although*** introduce an adverb clause.<br>(a) and (b) have the same meaning.  They mean:<br>*I was hungry, but I did not eat.* |
| COMPARE<br>(c) *Because*     I was hungry, *I ate.*<br>(d) *Even though* I was hungry, *I did not eat.* | *Because* expresses an expected result.<br>*Even though/although* expresses an unexpected or opposite result. |

# CHAPTER 9
## Comparisons

## CONTENTS

## 9-1   MAKING COMPARISONS WITH *AS . . . AS*

| | |
|---|---|
| (a) Tina is 21 years old.  Sam is also 21.<br>Tina is **as old as** Sam (is).<br><br>(b) Mike came **as quickly as** he could. | **As . . . as** is used to say that the two parts of a comparison are equal or the same in some way.<br>In (a): **as** + *adjective* + **as**<br>In (b): **as** + *adverb* + **as** |
| (c) Ted is 20.  Tina is 21.<br>Ted is **not as old as** Tina.<br>(d) Ted is**n't quite as** old **as** Tina.<br>(e) Amy is 5.  She is**n't nearly as** old **as** Tina. | Negative form: **not as . . . as.**★  **Quite** and **nearly** are often used with the negative.<br>In (d): **not quite as . . . as** = a small difference.<br>In (e): **not nearly as . . . as** = a big difference. |
| (f) Sam is **just as** old **as** Tina.<br>(g) Ted is **nearly/almost as** old **as** Tina. | Common modifiers of **as . . . as** are **just** (meaning "exactly") and **nearly/almost**. |

★Also possible: **not so . . . as**: *Ted is **not so** old **as** Tina.*

## 9-2 COMPARATIVE AND SUPERLATIVE

| | |
|---|---|
| (a) "A" is **older than** "B." <br> (b) "A" and "B" are **older than** "C" and "D." <br> (c) Ed is **more generous than** his brother. | The comparative compares *this* to *that* or *these* to *those*. Form: **-er** or **more**. (See Chart 9-3.) <br> Notice: A comparative is followed by **than**. |
| (d) "A," "B," "C," and "D" are sisters. "A" is **the oldest** of *all* four sisters. <br> (e) A woman in Turkey claims to be **the oldest person** in the world. <br> (f) Ed is **the most generous person** in his family. | The superlative compares one part of a whole group to all the rest of the group. Form: **-est** or **most**. (See Chart 9-3 for forms.) <br> Notice: A superlative begins with **the**. |

## 9-3 COMPARATIVE AND SUPERLATIVE FORMS OF ADJECTIVES AND ADVERBS

| | | COMPARATIVE | SUPERLATIVE | |
|---|---|---|---|---|
| ONE-SYLLABLE ADJECTIVES | old <br> wise | older <br> wiser | the oldest <br> the wisest | For most one-syllable adjectives, **-er** and **-est** are added. |
| TWO-SYLLABLE ADJECTIVES | famous <br> pleasant | more famous <br> more pleasant | the most famous <br> the most pleasant | For most two-syllable adjectives, **more** and **most** are used. |
| | busy <br> pretty | busier <br> prettier | the busiest <br> the prettiest | **-Er** and **-est** are used with two-syllable adjectives that end in *-y*. The *-y* is changed to *-i*. |
| | clever <br> <br> gentle <br> <br> friendly | cleverer <br> more clever <br> gentler <br> more gentle <br> friendlier <br> more friendly | the cleverest <br> the most clever <br> the gentlest <br> the most gentle <br> the friendliest <br> the most friendly | Some two-syllable adjectives use either **-er/-est** or **more/most**: *able, angry, clever, common, cruel, friendly, gentle, handsome, narrow, pleasant, polite, quiet, simple, sour.* |
| ADJECTIVES WITH THREE OR MORE SYLLABLES | important <br> fascinating | more important <br> more fascinating | the most important <br> the most fascinating | **More** and **most** are used with long adjectives. |
| IRREGULAR ADJECTIVES | good <br> bad | better <br> worse | the best <br> the worst | **Good** and **bad** have irregular comparative and superlative forms. |
| -LY ADVERBS | carefully <br> slowly | more carefully <br> more slowly | the most carefully <br> the most slowly | **More** and **most** are used with adverbs that end in **-ly**.★ |
| ONE-SYLLABLE ADVERBS | fast <br> hard | faster <br> harder | the fastest <br> the hardest | The **-er** and **-est** forms are used with one-syllable adverbs. |
| IRREGULAR ADVERBS | well <br> badly <br> far | better <br> worse <br> farther/further★★ | the best <br> the worst <br> the farthest/furthest | |

★Exception: **early** is both an adjective and an adverb. Forms: *earlier, earliest.*

★★Both **farther** and **further** are used to compare physical distances: *I walked farther/further than my friend did.* **Further** (but not **farther**) can also mean "additional": *I need further information.*

## 9-4 COMPLETING A COMPARATIVE

| | |
|---|---|
| (a) I'm older *than **my brother** (is)*. <br> (b) I'm older *than **he** is*. <br> (c) I'm older *than **him**. (informal)* | In formal English, a subject pronoun (e.g., *he*) follows ***than***, as in (b). In everyday, informal spoken English, an object pronoun (e.g., *him*) often follows ***than***, as in (c). |
| (d) He works harder *than **I do***. <br> (e) I arrived earlier *than **they did***. | Frequently an auxiliary verb follows the subject after ***than***. In (d): *than I do = than I work*. |
| (f) *Ann's* hair is longer *than **Kate's***. <br> (g) *Jack's* apartment is smaller *than **mine***. | A possessive noun (e.g., *Kate's*) or pronoun (e.g., *mine*) may follow ***than***. |

Ted is out of shape. I can run a lot
faster than **he can** OR (informally) **him**.

## 9-5 MODIFYING COMPARATIVES

| | |
|---|---|
| (a) Tom is ***very*** old. <br> (b) Ann drives ***very*** carefully. | ***Very*** often modifies adjectives, as in (a), and adverbs, as in (b). |
| (c) INCORRECT: *Tom is very older than I am.* <br>     INCORRECT: *Ann drives very more carefully <br>              than she used to.* | ***Very*** is NOT used to modify comparative adjectives and adverbs. |
| (d) Tom is ***much/a lot/far*** older than I am. <br> (e) Ann drives ***much/a lot/far*** more carefully <br>     than she used to. | Instead, ***much***, ***a lot***, or ***far*** are used to modify comparative adjectives and adverbs, as in (d) and (e). |
| (f) Ben is ***a little (bit)*** older than I am / OR <br>     *(informally)* me. | Another common modifier is ***a little/a little bit***, as in (f). |

## 9-6 COMPARISONS WITH *LESS . . . THAN* AND *NOT AS . . . AS*

| | |
|---|---|
| MORE THAN ONE SYLLABLE<br><br>(a) A pen is **less** *expensive* **than** a book.<br><br>(b) A pen is **not as** *expensive* **as** a book. | The opposite of **-er/more** is expressed by **less** or **not as . . . as**. (a) and (b) have the same meaning.<br><br>**Less** and **not as . . . as** are used with adjectives and adverbs of **more than one syllable**. |
| ONE SYLLABLE<br><br>(c) A pen is **not as** *large* **as** a book.<br><br>(d) *INCORRECT: A pen is less large than a book.* | Only **not as . . . as** (NOT **less**) is used with one-syllable adjectives or adverbs, as in (c). |

## 9-7 UNCLEAR COMPARISONS

| | |
|---|---|
| UNCLEAR<br>(a) Ann likes her dog better than her husband.<br><br>CLEAR<br>(b) Ann likes her dog better than her husband does.<br>(c) Ann likes her dog better than she does her husband. | Sometimes it is necessary to complete the idea following **than** in order to make a comparison clear.<br><br>In (b): *does* means "likes the dog."<br>In (c): *does* means "likes." |

## 9-8 USING *MORE* WITH NOUNS

| | |
|---|---|
| (a) Would you like some **more coffee**?<br>(b) Not everyone is here. I expect **more people** to come later. | In (a): *coffee* is a noun. When **more** is used with nouns, it often has the meaning of *additional*. It is not necessary to use **than**. |
| (c) There are **more people** in China **than** there are in the United States. | **More** is also used with nouns to make complete comparisons by adding **than**. |
| (d) Do you have enough coffee, or would you like some **more**? | When the meaning is clear, the noun may be omitted and **more** used by itself. |

## 9-9  REPEATING A COMPARATIVE

| | |
|---|---|
| (a) Because he was afraid, he walked **faster and faster**.<br>(b) Life in the modern world is becoming **more and more complex**. | Repeating a comparative gives the idea that something becomes progressively greater, i.e., it increases in intensity, quality, or quantity. |

The balloon got **bigger and bigger**.

## 9-10  USING DOUBLE COMPARATIVES

| | |
|---|---|
| (a) **The harder** you study, **the more** you will learn.<br>(b) **The more** she studied, **the more** she learned.<br>(c) **The warmer** the weather (is), **the better** I like it. | A double comparative has two parts; both parts begin with **the,** as in the examples. The second part of the comparison is the **result** of the first part.<br>In (a): If you study harder, the result will be that you will learn more. |
| (d) A: Should we ask Jenny and Jim to the party too?<br>   B: Why not? **The more, the merrier**.<br>(e) A: When should we leave?<br>   B: **The sooner, the better**. | **The more, the merrier** and **the sooner, the better** are two common expressions.<br>In (d): It is good to have more people at the party.<br>In (e): It is good if we leave as soon as we can. |

## 9-11  USING SUPERLATIVES

| | |
|---|---|
| (a) Tokyo is one of **the largest cities in the world**.<br>(b) David is **the most generous person I have ever known**.<br>(c) I have three books. These two are quite good, but this one is the **best** (book) **of all**. | Typical completions when a superlative is used:<br>In (a): superlative + *in* a place (*the world, this class, my family, the corporation, etc.*).<br>In (b): superlative + adjective clause.★<br>In (c): superlative + *of all*. |
| (d) I took four final exams. The final in accounting was **the least difficult** of all. | *The least* has the opposite meaning of *the most*. |
| (e) Ali is **one of** the best **students** in this class.<br>(f) **One of** the best **students** in this class **is** Ali. | Notice the pattern with **one of**:<br>   **one of** + PLURAL noun (+ SINGULAR verb) |

★See Chapter 12 for more information about adjective clauses.

## 9-12 USING *THE SAME, SIMILAR, DIFFERENT, LIKE, ALIKE*

| | |
|---|---|
| (a) John and Mary have **the same books**.<br>(b) John and Mary have **similar books**.<br>(c) John and Mary have **different books**.<br>(d) Their books are **the same**.<br>(e) Their books are **similar**.<br>(f) Their books are **different**. | **The same**, **similar**, and **different** are used as adjectives.<br>Notice: **the** always precedes **same**. |
| (g) This book is **the same as** that one.<br>(h) This book is **similar to** that one.<br>(i) This book is **different from** that one. | Notice: **the same** is followed by **as**;<br>    **similar** is followed by **to**;<br>    **different** is followed by **from**.* |
| (j) She is **the same age as** my mother.<br>    My shoes are **the same size as** yours. | A noun may come between **the same** and **as**, as in (j). |
| (k) My pen **is like** your pen.<br>(l) My pen and your pen **are alike**. | Notice in (k) and (l):<br>    *noun* + **be like** + *noun*<br>    *noun* and *noun* + **be alike** |
| (m) She **looks like** her sister.<br>    It **looks like** rain.<br>    It **sounds like** thunder.<br>    This material **feels like** silk.<br>    That **smells like** gas.<br>    This chemical **tastes like** salt.<br>    Stop **acting like** a fool.<br>    He **seems like** a nice fellow. | In addition to following **be**, **like** also follows certain verbs, primarily those dealing with the senses.<br>Notice the examples in (m). |
| (n) The twins **look alike**.<br>    We **think alike**.<br>    Most four-year-olds **act alike**.<br>    My sister and I **talk alike**.<br>    The little boys are **dressed alike**. | **Alike** may follow a few verbs other than **be**.<br>Notice the examples in (n). |

*In informal speech, native speakers might use **than** instead of **from** after **different**. **From** is considered correct in formal English, unless the comparison is completed by a clause: *I have a different attitude now than I used to have.*

No two zebras are exactly **alike**.
Even though Zee and Bee are **similar to**
each other, they are **different from** each other
in the exact pattern of their stripes.

# CHAPTER *10*
# The Passive

---

CONTENTS

---

## 10-1 ACTIVE SENTENCES AND PASSIVE SENTENCES

| | |
|---|---|
| (a) **ACTIVE:** The mouse *ate* the cheese.  (b) **PASSIVE:** The cheese *was eaten* by the mouse. | (a) and (b) have the same meaning. |

| ACTIVE | PASSIVE |
|---|---|
|  |  |

| | |
|---|---|
| **ACTIVE:**<br>**PASSIVE:**<br>(c) (d) 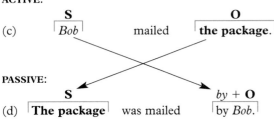 | In (c): The object in an active sentence becomes the subject in a passive sentence.<br><br>In (d): The subject in an active sentence is the object of *by* in the *by*-phrase in a passive sentence. |

## 10-2 FORM OF THE PASSIVE

| | BE | + | PAST PARTICIPLE | | Form of all passive verbs: |
|---|---|---|---|---|---|
| (a) Corn | *is* | | *grown* | by farmers. | **be** + *past participle* |
| (b) Sara | *was* | | *surprised* | by the news. | **Be** can be in any of its forms: *am, is, are, was, were,* |
| (c) The report | *will be* | | *written* | by Mary. | *has been, have been, will be, etc.* |

| | ACTIVE | PASSIVE |
|---|---|---|
| SIMPLE PRESENT | Farmers *grow* corn. ⟶ | Corn *is grown* by farmers. |
| SIMPLE PAST | The news *surprised* Sara. ⟶ | Sara *was surprised* by the news. |
| PRESENT PERFECT | Jack *has mailed* the letter. ⟶ | The letter *has been mailed* by Jack. |
| FUTURE | Mr. Lee *will plan* the meeting. ⟶ | The meeting *will be planned* by Mr. Lee. |
| | Sue *is going to write* the report. ⟶ | The report *is going to be written* by Sue. |

## 10-3 TRANSITIVE AND INTRANSITIVE VERBS

| | | | |
|---|---|---|---|
| (a) **TRANSITIVE** | | | A *transitive* verb is a verb that is followed by an object. |
| S | V | O | An object is a noun or a pronoun. |
| Bob | *mailed* | *the letter.* | |
| Mr. Lee | *signed* | *the check.* | |
| A cat | *killed* | *the bird.* | |
| (b) **INTRANSITIVE** | | | An *intransitive* verb is a verb that is not followed by an |
| S | V | | object. |
| An accident | *happened.* | | |
| Kate | *came* | to our house. | |
| I | *slept* | well last night. | |

COMMON INTRANSITIVE VERBS*

| | | | | |
|---|---|---|---|---|
| *agree* | *die* | *happen* | *rise* | *stand* |
| *appear* | *exist* | *laugh* | *seem* | *stay* |
| *arrive* | *fall* | *live* | *sit* | *talk* |
| *become* | *flow* | *occur* | *sleep* | *wait* |
| *come* | *go* | *rain* | *sneeze* | *walk* |

| | |
|---|---|
| (c) **TRANSITIVE VERBS** <br> ACTIVE: Bob *mailed* the letter. <br> PASSIVE: The letter *was mailed* by Bob. | Only transitive verbs can be used in the passive. |
| (d) **INTRANSITIVE VERBS** <br> ACTIVE: An accident *happened.* <br> PASSIVE: *(not possible)* <br> (e) *INCORRECT:* An accident *was happened.* | An intransitive verb is NOT used in the passive. |

*To find out if a verb is transitive or intransitive, look in your dictionary. The usual abbreviations are v.t. (transitive) and v.i. (intransitive). Some verbs have both transitive and intransitive uses. For example:

    transitive: *Students study books.*
    intransitive: *Students study.*

## 10-4 USING THE *BY*-PHRASE

| | |
|---|---|
| (a) This sweater *was made* **by my aunt**. | The *by*-phrase is used in passive sentences when it is important to know who performs an action. In (a): *by my aunt* is important information. |
| (b) My sweater *was made* in Korea.<br>(c) Spanish *is spoken* in Colombia.<br>(d) That house *was built* in 1940.<br>(e) Rice *is grown* in many countries. | Usually there is no *by*-phrase in a passive sentence. The passive is used when it is **not known or not important to know exactly who performs an action**.<br>In (b): The exact person (or people) who made the sweater is not known and is not important to know, so there is no *by*-phrase in the passive sentence. |
| (f) **My aunt** is very skillful. **She** *made* this sweater.<br><br>(g) — I like your sweaters.<br>—Thanks. **This sweater** *was made by* my aunt. **That sweater** *was made by* my mother. | Usually the active is used when the speaker knows who performed the action, as in (f), where the focus of attention is on *my aunt*.<br>In (g), the speaker uses the passive WITH a *by*-phrase because he wants to focus attention on the subjects of the sentences. The focus of attention is on the two sweaters. The *by*-phrases add important information. |

## 10-5 THE PASSIVE FORMS OF THE PRESENT AND PAST PROGRESSIVE

| ACTIVE | PASSIVE | |
|---|---|---|
| The secretary *is copying* some letters.<br>Someone *is building* a new hospital. | (a) Some letters *are being copied* by the secretary.<br>(b) A new hospital *is being built*. | Passive form of the present progressive:<br>$\left.\begin{array}{l} \textit{am} \\ \textit{is} \\ \textit{are} \end{array}\right\}$ + ***being*** + *past participle* |
| The secretary *was copying* some letters.<br>Someone *was building* a new hospital. | (c) Some letters *were being copied* by the secretary.<br>(d) A new hospital *was being built*. | Passive form of the past progressive:<br>$\left.\begin{array}{l} \textit{was} \\ \textit{were} \end{array}\right\}$ + ***being*** + *past participle* |

PASSIVE: The swimmer ***is being asked*** for the time by a fish!

## 10-6 PASSIVE MODAL AUXILIARIES

| ACTIVE MODAL AUXILIARIES | PASSIVE MODAL AUXILIARIES (MODAL + *BE* + PAST PARTICIPLE) | | Modal auxiliaries are often used in the passive. |
|---|---|---|---|
| Bob *will mail* it. | It | *will be mailed* by Bob. | FORM: *modal* + *be* + *past participle* |
| Bob *can mail* it. | It | *can be mailed* by Bob. | (See Chapter 7 for information about |
| Bob *should mail* it. | It | *should be mailed* by Bob. | the meanings and uses of modal |
| Bob *ought to mail* it. | It | *ought to be mailed* by Bob. | auxiliaries.) |
| Bob *must mail* it. | It | *must be mailed* by Bob. | |
| Bob *has to mail* it. | It | *has to be mailed* by Bob. | |
| Bob *may mail* it. | It | *may be mailed* by Bob. | |
| Bob *might mail* it. | It | *might be mailed* by Bob. | |
| Bob *could mail* it. | It | *could be mailed* by Bob. | |

## 10-7 USING PAST PARTICIPLES AS ADJECTIVES (STATIVE PASSIVE)

| | *BE* + ADJECTIVE | | *Be* can be followed by an adjective. The adjective describes or gives information about the subject of the sentence. |
|---|---|---|---|
| (a) Paul | *is* | *young*. | |
| (b) Paul | *is* | *tall*. | *Be* can be followed by a past participle (the passive |
| (c) Paul | *is* | *hungry*. | form). The past participle is often like an adjective. The |
| | *BE* + PAST PARTICIPLE | | past participle describes or gives information about the |
| (d) Paul | *is* | *married*. | subject of the sentence. Past participles are used as |
| (e) Paul | *is* | *tired*. | adjectives in many common, everyday expressions. |
| (f) Paul | *is* | *frightened*. | |

| | |
|---|---|
| (g) Paul *is married **to** Susan.* | Often the past participles in these expressions are |
| (h) Paul *was excited **about** the game.* | followed by particular prepositions + an object. |
| (i) Paul *will be prepared **for** the exam.* | For example: |
| | *married* is followed by *to* (+ an object) |
| | *excited* is followed by *about* (+ an object) |
| | *prepared* is followed by *for* (+ an object) |

SOME COMMON EXPRESSIONS WITH *BE* + PAST PARTICIPLE

| | | |
|---|---|---|
| 1. *be acquainted (with)* | 13. *be excited (about)* | 25. *be opposed (to)* |
| 2. *be bored (with, by)* | 14. *be exhausted (from)* | 26. *be pleased (with)* |
| 3. *be broken* | 15. *be finished (with)* | 27. *be prepared (for)* |
| 4. *be closed* | 16. *be frightened (of, by)* | 28. *be qualified (for)* |
| 5. *be composed of* | 17. *be gone (from)* | 29. *be related (to)* |
| 6. *be crowded (with)* | 18. *be hurt* | 30. *be satisfied (with)* |
| 7. *be devoted (to)* | 19. *be interested (in)* | 31. *be scared (of, by)* |
| 8. *be disappointed (in, with)* | 20. *be involved (in, with)* | 32. *be shut* |
| 9. *be divorced (from)* | 21. *be located in, south of, etc.* | 33. *be spoiled* |
| 10. *be done (with)* | 22. *be lost* | 34. *be terrified (of, by)* |
| 11. *be drunk (on)* | 23. *be made of* | 35. *be tired (of, from)★* |
| 12. *be engaged (to)* | 24. *be married (to)* | 36. *be worried (about)* |

★I'm **tired *of*** the cold weather. = *I've had enough cold weather. I want the weather to get warm.*
I'm **tired *from*** working hard all day. = *I'm exhausted because I worked hard all day.*

## 10-8 PARTICIPIAL ADJECTIVES: *-ED* vs. *-ING*

| | |
|---|---|
| **Indian art interests me.**<br><br>(a) I am ***interested*** in Indian art.<br>    INCORRECT: *I am interesting in Indian art.*<br><br>(b) Indian art is ***interesting***.<br>    INCORRECT: *Indian art is interested.*<br><br>**The news surprised Kate.**<br>(c) Kate was ***surprised***.<br>(d) The news was ***surprising***. | The past participle *(-ed)*★ and the present participle *(-ing)* can be used as adjectives.<br>In (a): The past participle *(interested)* describes how a person feels.<br>In (b): The present participle *(interesting)* describes the **cause** of the feeling. The cause of the interest is Indian art.<br><br>In (c): *surprised* describes how Kate felt.<br>The past participle carries a passive meaning: *Kate was surprised* **by the news**.<br>In (d): *the news* was the cause of the surprise. |
| (e) Did you hear the ***surprising news?***<br>(f) Roberto fixed the ***broken window***. | Like other adjectives, participial adjectives may follow *be*, as in examples (a) through (d), or come in front of nouns, as in (e) and (f). |

★ The past participle of regular verbs ends in *-ed*. Some verbs have irregular forms. See Chart 2-6, p. 9.

## 10-9 *GET* + ADJECTIVE; *GET* + PAST PARTICIPLE

| | |
|---|---|
| ***GET*** + **ADJECTIVE**<br>(a) I ***am getting hungry***. Let's eat.<br>(b) Eric ***got nervous*** before the job interview. | ***Get*** can be followed by an adjective. ***Get*** gives the idea of change—the idea of becoming, beginning to be, growing to be.<br>In (a): *I'm getting hungry.* = *I wasn't hungry before, but now I'm beginning to be hungry.* |
| ***GET*** + **PAST PARTICIPLE**<br>(c) I'm ***getting tired***. Let's stop working.<br>(d) Steve and Rita ***got married*** last month. | Sometimes ***get*** is followed by a past participle. The past participle after ***get*** is like an adjective; it describes the subject of the sentence. |

| ***GET*** + **ADJECTIVE** | | | ***GET*** + **PAST PARTICIPLE** | | |
|---|---|---|---|---|---|
| get angry | get dry | get quiet | get acquainted | get drunk | get involved |
| get bald | get fat | get rich | get arrested | get engaged | get killed |
| get big | get full | get serious | get bored | get excited | get lost |
| get busy | get hot | get sick | get confused | get finished | get married |
| get close | get hungry | get sleepy | get crowded | get frightened | get scared |
| get cold | get interested | get thirsty | get divorced | get hurt | get sunburned |
| get dark | get late | get well | get done | get interested | get tired |
| get dirty | get nervous | get wet | get dressed | get invited | get worried |
| get dizzy | get old | | | | |

## 10-10 USING *BE USED/ACCUSTOMED TO* AND *GET USED/ACCUSTOMED TO*

| | |
|---|---|
| (a) I **am used to** hot weather.<br>(b) I **am accustomed to** hot weather.<br><br>(c) I *am used* **to** *living* in a hot climate.<br>(d) I *am accustomed* **to** *living* in a hot climate. | (a) and (b) have the same meaning: "Living in a hot climate is usual and normal for me. I'm familiar with what it is like to live in a hot climate. Hot weather isn't strange or different to me."<br><br>Notice in (c) and (d): *to* (a preposition) is followed by the *-ing* form of a verb (a gerund). |
| (e) I just moved from Florida to Siberia. I have never lived in a cold climate before, but I **am getting used to** *(accustomed to)* the cold weather here. | In (e): *I'm getting used to/accustomed to* = something is beginning to seem usual and normal to me. |

## 10-11 *USED TO* vs. *BE USED TO*

| | |
|---|---|
| (a) I *used to* **live** in Chicago, but now I live in Tokyo.<br>INCORRECT: *I used to living in Chicago.*<br>INCORRECT: *I am used to live in a big city.* | In (a): *Used to* expresses the habitual past (see Chart 2-11, p. 13). It is followed by the **simple form of a verb**. |
| (b) I *am used to* **living** in a big city. | In (b): *be used to* is followed by the *-ing* form of a verb (a gerund).* |

*NOTE: In both *used to* (habitual past) and *be used to*, the "d" is not pronounced in *used*.

## 10-12 USING *BE SUPPOSED TO*

| | |
|---|---|
| (a) Mike *is supposed to call* me tomorrow.<br>(IDEA: I expect Mike to call me tomorrow.)<br><br>(b) We *are supposed to write* a composition.<br>(IDEA: The teacher expects us to write a composition.) | *Be supposed to* is used to talk about an activity or event that is expected to occur.<br><br>In (a): The idea of *is supposed to* is that Mike is expected (by me) to call me. I asked him to call me. He promised to call me. I expect him to call me. |
| (c) Alice *was supposed to be* home at ten, but she didn't get in until midnight.<br>(IDEA: Someone expected Alice to be home at ten.) | In the past form, *be supposed to* often expresses the idea that an expected event did not occur, as in (c). |

# CHAPTER 11

## Count/Noncount Nouns and Articles

## 11-1  *A* vs. *AN*

| | |
|---|---|
| (a) I have *a **p**encil*. <br> (b) I live in *an **a**partment*. <br><br> (c) I have *a **s**mall apartment*. <br> (d) I live in *an **o**ld building*. | *A* and *an* are used in front of a singular noun (e.g., *pencil, apartment*). They mean "one." <br> If a singular noun is modified by an adjective (e.g., *small, old* ), *a* or *an* comes in front of the adjective, as in (c) and (d). <br> *A* is used in front of words that begin with a consonant (*b, c, d, f, g, etc.*): *a boy, a bad day, a cat, a cute baby*. <br> *An* is used in front of words that begin with the vowels *a*, *e*, *i*, and *o*: *an apartment, an angry man, an elephant, an empty room, etc.* |
| (e) I have *an **u**mbrella*. <br> (f) I saw *an **u**gly picture*. <br><br> (g) I attend *a **u**niversity*. <br> (h) I had *a **u**nique experience*. | For words that begin with the letter *u*: <br>   (1) *An* is used if the *u* is a vowel sound, as in *an umbrella, an uncle, an unusual day*. <br>   (2) *A* is used if the *u* is a consonant sound, as in *a university, a unit, a usual event*. |
| (i) He will arrive in *an **h**our*. <br> (j) New Year's Day is *a **h**oliday*. | For words that begin with the letter *h*: <br>   (1) *An* is used if the *h* is silent: *an hour, an honor, an honest person*. <br>   (2) *A* is used if the *h* is pronounced: *a holiday, a hotel, a high point*. |

## 11-2 COUNT AND NONCOUNT NOUNS

| | SINGULAR | | PLURAL | | A count noun: |
|---|---|---|---|---|---|
| COUNT NOUN | *a* <br> *one* | chair <br> chair | Ø* <br> *two* <br> *some* | chairs <br> chairs <br> chairs | (1) can be counted with numbers: *one chair, two chairs, ten chairs, etc.* <br> (2) can be preceded by *a/an* in the singular: *a chair.* <br> (3) has a plural form ending in *-s* or *-es: chairs.*\*\* |
| NONCOUNT NOUN | Ø <br> *some* | furniture <br> furniture | Ø <br> Ø | | A noncount noun: <br> (1) cannot be counted with numbers. <br>    *INCORRECT: one furniture* <br> (2) is NOT immediately preceded by *a/an*. <br>    *INCORRECT: a furniture* <br> (3) does NOT have a plural form (no final-*s*). <br>    *INCORRECT: furnitures* |

\*Ø = "nothing."
\*\*See Chart 1-5, p. 4, and Chart 6-1, p. 38, for the spelling and pronunciation of *-s/-es*.

## 11-3 NONCOUNT NOUNS

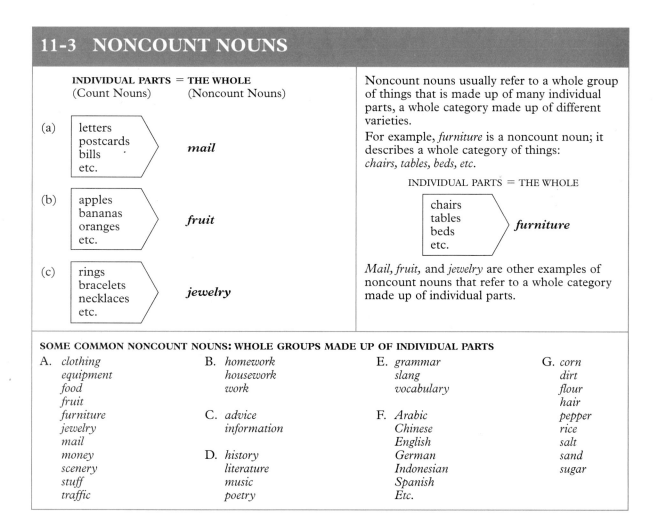

INDIVIDUAL PARTS = THE WHOLE
(Count Nouns)          (Noncount Nouns)

(a) letters / postcards / bills / etc. → *mail*

(b) apples / bananas / oranges / etc. → *fruit*

(c) rings / bracelets / necklaces / etc. → *jewelry*

Noncount nouns usually refer to a whole group of things that is made up of many individual parts, a whole category made up of different varieties.

For example, *furniture* is a noncount noun; it describes a whole category of things: *chairs, tables, beds, etc.*

INDIVIDUAL PARTS = THE WHOLE

chairs / tables / beds / etc. → *furniture*

*Mail, fruit,* and *jewelry* are other examples of noncount nouns that refer to a whole category made up of individual parts.

### SOME COMMON NONCOUNT NOUNS: WHOLE GROUPS MADE UP OF INDIVIDUAL PARTS

| A. *clothing* <br> *equipment* <br> *food* <br> *fruit* <br> *furniture* <br> *jewelry* <br> *mail* <br> *money* <br> *scenery* <br> *stuff* <br> *traffic* | B. *homework* <br> *housework* <br> *work* <br><br> C. *advice* <br> *information* <br><br> D. *history* <br> *literature* <br> *music* <br> *poetry* | E. *grammar* <br> *slang* <br> *vocabulary* <br><br> F. *Arabic* <br> *Chinese* <br> *English* <br> *German* <br> *Indonesian* <br> *Spanish* <br> *Etc.* | G. *corn* <br> *dirt* <br> *flour* <br> *hair* <br> *pepper* <br> *rice* <br> *salt* <br> *sand* <br> *sugar* |
|---|---|---|---|

## 11-4 MORE NONCOUNT NOUNS

| (a) LIQUIDS | | SOLIDS and SEMI-SOLIDS | | | | GASES |
|---|---|---|---|---|---|---|
| coffee | soup | bread | meat | chalk | paper | air |
| milk | tea | butter | beef | glass | soap | pollution |
| oil | water | cheese | chicken | gold | toothpaste | smog |
| | | ice | fish | iron | wood | smoke |

(b) THINGS THAT OCCUR IN NATURE

| weather | darkness | thunder |
|---|---|---|
| rain | light | lightning |
| snow | sunshine | |

(c) ABSTRACTIONS*

| beauty | fun | health | ignorance | patience | time |
|---|---|---|---|---|---|
| courage | generosity | help | knowledge | progress | violence |
| experience | happiness | honesty | luck | | |

*An abstraction is an idea. It has no physical form. A person cannot touch it.

## 11-5 USING *SEVERAL, A LOT OF, MANY/MUCH,* AND *A FEW/A LITTLE*

| | COUNT | NONCOUNT | |
|---|---|---|---|
| (a) | *several* chairs | Ø | *Several* is used only with *count* nouns. |
| (b) | *a lot of* chairs | *a lot of* furniture | *A lot of* is used with both *count* and *noncount* nouns. |
| (c) | *many* chairs | *much* furniture | *Many* is used with *count* nouns.<br>*Much* is used with *noncount* nouns. |
| (d) | *a few* chairs | *a little* furniture | *A few* is used with *count* nouns.<br>*A little* is used with *noncount* nouns. |

## 11-6  NOUNS THAT CAN BE COUNT OR NONCOUNT

Quite a few nouns can be used as either count or noncount nouns.  Examples of both count and noncount usages for some common nouns follow.

| NOUN | USED AS A **NONCOUNT** NOUN | USED AS A **COUNT** NOUN |
|---|---|---|
| *glass* | (a)  Windows are made of ***glass***. | (b)  I drank ***a glass*** of water.<br>(c)  Janet wears ***glasses*** when she reads. |
| *hair* | (d)  Rita has brown ***hair***. | (e)  There's ***a hair*** on my jacket. |
| *iron* | (f )  ***Iron*** is a metal. | (g)  I pressed my shirt with ***an iron***. |
| *light* | (h)  I opened the curtain to let in ***some light***. | (i)  Please turn off ***the lights*** *(lamps)*. |
| *paper* | (j)  I need ***some paper*** to write a letter. | (k)  I wrote ***a paper*** for Professor Lee.<br>(l)  I bought ***a paper*** *(a newspaper)*. |
| *time* | (m)  How ***much time*** do you need to finish your work? | (n)  How ***many times*** have you been in Mexico? |
| *work* | (o)  I have ***some work*** to do tonight. | (p)  That painting is ***a work*** of art. |
| *coffee* | (q)  I had ***some coffee*** after dinner. | (r)  ***Two coffees***, please. |
| *chicken/ fish* | (s)  I ate ***some chicken/some fish***. | (t)  She drew a picture of ***a chicken/a fish***. |
| *experience* | (u)  I haven't had ***much experience*** with computers. (I don't have much knowledge or skill in using computers.) | (v)  I had ***many*** interesting ***experiences*** on my trip.  (Many interesting events happened to me on my trip.) |

## 11-7  USING UNITS OF MEASURE WITH NONCOUNT NOUNS

| | |
|---|---|
| (a)  I had some tea.<br>(b)  I had ***two cups of*** tea.<br>(c)  I ate some toast.<br>(d)  I ate ***one piece of*** toast. | To mention a specific quantity of a noncount noun, speakers use units of measure such as *two cups of* or *one piece of*.  A unit of measure usually describes **the container** *(a cup of, a bowl of )*, **the amount** *(a pound of, a quart of )*,\* or **the shape** *(a bar of soap, a sheet of paper)*. |

\*Weight measure: *one pound* = 0.45 kilograms/kilos.
  Liquid measure: *one quart* = 0.95 litres/liters; four quarts = one gallon = 3.8 litres/liters.

|  | USING *A* OR Ø (NO ARTICLE) | | USING *A* OR *SOME* |
|---|---|---|---|
| **SINGULAR COUNT NOUNS** | (a) *A dog* makes a good pet.<br>(b) *A banana* is yellow.<br>(c) *A pencil* contains lead. | A speaker uses *a* with a singular count noun when s/he is making a generalization.<br><br>In (a): The speaker is talking about any dog, all dogs, dogs in general. | (j) I saw *a dog* in my yard.<br>(k) Mary ate *a banana*.<br>(l) I need *a pencil*. |
| **PLURAL COUNT NOUNS** | (d) Ø *Dogs* make good pets.<br>(e) Ø *Bananas* are yellow.<br>(f) Ø *Pencils* contain lead. | A speaker uses no article (Ø) with a plural count noun when s/he is making a generalization.★<br>In (d): The speaker is talking about any dog, all dogs, dogs in general.<br>Note: (a) and (d) have the same meaning. | (m) I saw **some dogs** in my yard.<br>(n) Mary bought **some bananas**.<br>(o) Bob has **some pencils** in his pocket. |
| **NONCOUNT NOUNS** | (g) Ø *Fruit* is good for you.<br>(h) Ø *Coffee* contains caffeine.<br>(i) I like Ø *music*. | A speaker uses no article (Ø) with a noncount noun when s/he is making a generalization.<br>In (g): The speaker is talking about any fruit, all fruit, fruit in general. | (p) I bought **some fruit**.<br>(q) Bob drank **some coffee**.<br>(r) Would you like to listen to **some music**? |

★Sometimes a speaker uses an expression of quantity (e.g., **almost all, most, some**) when s/he makes a generalization:
*Almost all dogs make good pets. Most dogs are friendly. Some dogs have short hair.*

| | USING *THE* | |
|---|---|---|
| A speaker uses *a* with a singular count noun when s/he is talking about one thing (or person) that is not specific.<br><br>In (j): The speaker is saying, "I saw one dog (not two dogs, some dogs, many dogs). It wasn't a specific dog (e.g., your dog, the neighbor's dog, that dog). It was only one dog out of the whole group of animals called dogs." | (s) Did you feed *the dog?*<br>(t) I had a banana and an apple. I gave *the banana* to Mary.<br>(u) *The pencil* on that desk is Jim's.<br>(v) *The sun* is shining.<br>(w) Please close *the door*.<br>(x) Mary is in *the kitchen*. | *The* is used in front of<br>(1) singular count nouns: *the dog*.<br>(2) plural count nouns: *the dogs*.<br>(3) noncount nouns: *the fruit*.<br><br>A speaker uses *the* (not *a, Ø*, or *some*) when the speaker and the listener are thinking about the same specific person(s) or thing(s). |
| A speaker often uses *some** with a plural count noun when s/he is talking about things (or people) that are not specific.<br><br>In (m): The speaker is saying, "I saw more than one dog. They weren't specific dogs (e.g., your dogs, the neighbor's dogs, those dogs). The exact number of dogs isn't important (two dogs, five dogs); I'm simply saying that I saw an indefinite number of dogs." | (y) Did you feed *the dogs?*<br>(z) I had some bananas and apples. I gave *the bananas* to Mary.<br>(aa) *The pencils* on that desk are Jim's.<br>(bb) Please turn off *the lights*. | In (s): The speaker and the listener are thinking about the same specific dog. The listener knows which dog the speaker is talking about: the dog that they own, the dog that they feed every day. There is only one dog that the speaker could possibly be talking about.<br><br>In (t): A speaker uses *the* when s/he mentions a noun the second time.<br>First mention:<br>*I had **a banana** . . . .*<br>Second mention:<br>*I gave **the banana** . . . .*<br>In the second mention, the listener now knows which banana the speaker is talking about: the banana the speaker had (not the banana John had, not the banana in that bowl). |
| A speaker often uses *some** with a noncount noun when s/he is talking about something that is not specific.<br><br>In (p): The speaker is saying, "I bought an indefinite amount of fruit. The exact amount (e.g., two pounds of fruit, four bananas, and two apples) isn't important. And I'm not talking about specific fruit (e.g., that fruit, the fruit in that bowl.)" | (cc) *The fruit* in this bowl is ripe.<br>(dd) I drank some coffee and some milk. *The coffee* was hot.<br>(ee) I can't hear you. *The music* is too loud.<br>(ff) *The air* is cold today. | |

*In addition to *some*, a speaker might use *several, a few, a lot of*, *etc.*, with a plural count noun, or *a little, a lot of*, *etc.*, with a noncount noun. (See Chart 11-5, p. 74.)

| | |
|---|---|
| (a) We met **Ø** *Mr. Wang.*<br>I know **Ø** *Doctor Smith.*<br>**Ø** *President Rice* has been in the news. | ***The*** is NOT used with titled names.<br>*INCORRECT: We met the Mr. Wang.* |
| (b) He lives in **Ø** *Europe.*<br>**Ø** *Asia* is the largest continent.<br>Have you ever been in **Ø** *Africa?* | ***The*** is NOT used with the names of continents.<br>*INCORRECT: He lives in the Europe.* |
| (c) He lives in **Ø** *France.*<br>**Ø** *Brazil* is a large country.<br>Have you ever been in **Ø** *Thailand?* | ***The*** is NOT used with the names of most countries.<br>*INCORRECT: He lives in the France.* |
| (d) He lives in *the* **United States.**<br>*The* **Netherlands** is in Europe.<br>Have you ever been in *the* **Philippines?** | ***The*** is used in the names of only a few countries, as in the examples. Others: *the Czech Republic, the United Arab Emirates, the Dominican Republic.* |
| (e) He lives in **Ø** *Paris.*<br>**Ø** *New York* is the largest city in the United States<br>Have you ever been in **Ø** *Istanbul?* | ***The*** is NOT used with the names of cities.<br>*INCORRECT: He lives in the Paris.* |
| (f) *The* **Nile River** is long.<br>They crossed *the* **Pacific Ocean.**<br>*The* **Yellow Sea** is in Asia.<br>(g) Chicago is on **Ø** *Lake Michigan.*<br>**Ø** *Lake Titicaca* lies on the border between Peru and Bolivia. | ***The*** is used with the names of rivers, oceans, and seas.<br><br>***The*** is NOT used with the names of lakes. |
| (h) We hiked in *the* **Alps.**<br>*The* **Andes** are in South America.<br>(i) He climbed **Ø** *Mount Everest.*<br>**Ø** *Mount Fuji* is in Japan. | ***The*** is used with the names of mountain ranges.<br><br>***The*** is NOT used with the names of individual mountains. |

**Florida, California,** and **North Dakota**
are the largest producers of honey
in **the United States.**

## 11-10 CAPITALIZATION

| CAPITALIZE | | |
|---|---|---|
| 1. The first word of a sentence | (a) **W**e saw a movie last night.<br>**I**t was very good. | *Capitalize* = use a big letter, not a small letter. |
| 2. The names of people | (b) I met **G**eorge **A**dams yesterday. | |
| 3. Titles used with the names of people | (c) I saw **D**octor (**D**r.) Smith.<br>Do you know **P**rofessor (**P**rof.) Alston? | COMPARE<br>I saw a **d**octor.<br>I saw **D**octor Wilson. |
| 4. Months, days, holidays | (d) I was born in **A**pril.<br>Bob arrived last **M**onday.<br>It snowed on **T**hanksgiving **D**ay. | NOTE: Seasons are not capitalized:<br>*spring, summer, fall/autumn, winter* |
| 5. The names of places:<br>city<br>state/province<br>country<br>continent | (e) He lives in **C**hicago.<br>She was born in **C**alifornia.<br>They are from **M**exico.<br>Tibet is in **A**sia. | COMPARE<br>She lives in a **c**ity.<br>She lives in **N**ew **Y**ork City. |
| ocean<br>lake<br>river<br>desert<br>mountain | They crossed the **A**tlantic **O**cean.<br>Chicago is on **L**ake **M**ichigan.<br>The **N**ile **R**iver flows north.<br>The **S**ahara **D**esert is in Africa.<br>We visited the **R**ocky **M**ountains. | COMPARE<br>They crossed a **r**iver.<br>They crossed the **Y**ellow **R**iver. |
| school<br>business | I go to the **U**niversity of **F**lorida.<br>I work for the **G**eneral **E**lectric **C**ompany. | COMPARE<br>I go to a **u**niversity.<br>I go to the **U**niversity of **T**exas. |
| street<br>building<br>park, zoo | He lives on **G**rand **A**venue.<br>We have class in **R**itter **H**all.<br>I went jogging in **F**orest **P**ark. | COMPARE<br>We went to a **p**ark.<br>We went to **C**entral **P**ark. |
| 6. The names of courses | (f) I'm taking **C**hemistry 101 this term. | COMPARE<br>I'm reading a book about **p**sychology.<br>I'm taking **P**sychology 101 this term. |
| 7. The titles of books, articles, movies | (g) *Gone with the Wind*<br>*The Old Man and the Sea* | Capitalize the first word of a title. Capitalize all other words except articles *(the, a/an)*, coordinating conjunctions *(and, but, or)*, and short prepositions *(with, in, at, etc.)*. |
| 8. The names of languages and nationalities | (h) She speaks **S**panish.<br>We discussed **J**apanese customs. | Words that refer to the names of nations, nationalities, and languages are always capitalized. |
| 9. The names of religions | (i) **B**uddism, **C**hristianity, **H**induism, **I**slam, and **J**udaism are major religions in the world.<br>Talal is a **M**oslem. | Words that refer to the names of religions are always capitalized. |
| 10. The pronoun "I" | (j) Yesterday **I** fell off my bicycle. | The pronoun "I" is always capitalized. |

# CHAPTER 12
# Adjective Clauses

## CONTENTS

## 12-1  ADJECTIVE CLAUSES: INTRODUCTION

| ADJECTIVES | ADJECTIVE CLAUSES |
|---|---|
| An **adjective** modifies a noun. "Modify" means to change a little. An adjective describes or gives information about the noun. (See Chart 6-8, p. 43.) | An **adjective clause*** modifies a noun. It describes or gives information about a noun. |
| An adjective usually comes in front of a noun. | An adjective clause follows a noun. |

|  |  |
|---|---|
| (a) I met a *adjective* **kind** + *noun* man.  (b) I met a *adjective* **famous** + *noun* man. | (c) I met a *noun* man + *adjective clause* **who is kind to everybody.**  (d) I met a *noun* man + *adjective clause* **who is a famous poet.**  (e) I met a *noun* man + *adjective clause* **who lives in Chicago.** |

| *GRAMMAR TERMINOLOGY | |
|---|---|
| (1) *I met a man* = an independent clause; it is a complete sentence.  (2) *He lives in Chicago* = an independent clause; it is a complete sentence.  (3) *who lives in Chicago* = a dependent clause; it is NOT a complete sentence.  (4) *I met a man who lives in Chicago* = an independent clause + a dependent clause; a complete sentence. | A **clause** is a structure that has a subject and a verb. There are two kinds of clauses: **independent** and **dependent**.  • An **independent clause** is a main clause and can stand alone as a sentence.  • A **dependent clause** cannot stand alone as a sentence; it must be connected to an independent clause. |

## 12-2 USING *WHO* AND *WHOM* IN ADJECTIVE CLAUSES

| | | |
|---|---|---|
| (a) The man is friendly. | S     V<br>*He* lives next to me.<br>↓<br>*who*<br>↓<br>S     V<br>*who* lives next to me | In (a): *He* is a subject pronoun. *He* refers to "the man."<br>To make an adjective clause, change *he* to *who*. *Who* is a subject pronoun. *Who* refers to "the man." |
| (b) The man   *who lives next to me*   is friendly. | | In (b): An adjective clause immediately follows the noun it modifies.<br>*INCORRECT: The man is friendly who lives next to me.* |
| (c) The man was friendly. | S  V   O<br>I  met *him*.<br>↓<br>———— *whom*<br>↓<br>O    S  V<br>*whom* I met | In (c): *him* is an object pronoun. *Him* refers to "the man."<br>To make an adjective clause, change *him* to *whom*. *Whom* is an object pronoun. *Whom* refers to "the man." *Whom* comes at the beginning of an adjective clause. |
| (d) The man   *whom I met*   was friendly. | | In (d): An adjective clause immediately follows the noun it modifies.<br>*INCORRECT: The man was friendly whom I met.* |

## 12-3 USING *WHO, WHO(M)*, AND *THAT* IN ADJECTIVE CLAUSES

| | | |
|---|---|---|
| (a) The man is friendly. | S     V<br>*He* lives next to me.<br>↓<br>*who*<br>*that* | In addition to *who, that* can be used as the subject of an adjective clause.<br>(b) and (c) have the same meaning. |
| S    V<br>(b) The man *who lives next to me* is friendly.<br>(c) The man *that lives next to me* is friendly. | | A subject pronoun cannot be omitted:<br>*INCORRECT: The man lives next to me is friendly.*<br>  *CORRECT: The man who/that lives next to me is friendly.* |
| | S V | In addition to *who(m)*,★ *that* can be used as the object in an adjective clause. |
| (d) The man was friendly. I met | O<br>*him.*<br>↓<br>*whom*<br>*that* | (e) and (f) have the same meaning. |
| O     S V<br>(e) The man  *who(m)*  *I met*  was friendly.<br>(f) The man  *that*    *I met*  was friendly.<br>(g) The man  Ø      *I met*  was friendly. | | An object pronoun can be omitted from an adjective clause. (e), (f), and (g) have the same meaning.<br>In (g): The symbol "Ø" means "nothing goes here." |

★The parentheses around the "m" in *who(m)* indicate that (especially in everyday conversation) *who* is often used as an object pronoun instead of the more formal *whom*.

## 12-4 USING *WHICH* AND *THAT* IN ADJECTIVE CLAUSES

| | |
|---|---|
| (a) The river is polluted. <br><br> **S**    V <br> **It**     flows through the town. <br> ↓ <br> *which* <br> *that* <br><br>       **S**    V <br> (b) The river   ***which*** *flows through the town*   is polluted. <br> (c) The river   ***that***   *flows through the town*   is polluted. | ***Who*** and ***whom*** refer to people. ***Which*** refers to things. ***That*** can refer to either people or things. |
| | In (a): To make an adjective clause, change ***it*** to ***which*** or ***that***. ***It***, ***which***, and ***that*** all refer to a thing (the river). <br> (b) and (c) have the same meaning. |
| | When ***which*** and ***that*** are used as the subject of an adjective clause, they CANNOT be omitted. <br> *INCORRECT: The river flows through town is polluted.* |
|      **S**    V      **O** <br> (d) The books were expensive. I bought   ***them.*** <br> ↓ <br> *which* <br> *that* <br><br>      **O**    **S** V <br> (e) The books   ***which***   *I bought*   were expensive. <br> (f) The books   ***that***   *I bought*   were expensive. <br> (g) The books   **Ø**     *I bought*   were expensive. | ***Which*** or ***that*** can be used as an object in an adjective clause, as in (e) and (f). |
| | An object pronoun can be omitted from an adjective clause, as in (g). <br> (e), (f), and (g) have the same meaning. |

## 12-5 SINGULAR AND PLURAL VERBS IN ADJECTIVE CLAUSES

| | |
|---|---|
| (a) I know the **man** *who **is** sitting over there.* | In (a): The verb in the adjective clause *(is)* is singular because ***who*** refers to a singular noun, *man*. |
| (b) I know the **people** *who **are** sitting over there.* | In (b): The verb in the adjective clause *(are)* is plural because ***who*** refers to a plural noun, *people*. |

The woman *who **was** sitting in front of me at the movie* was wearing a big hat.

## 12-6　USING PREPOSITIONS IN ADJECTIVE CLAUSES

| | | | | | |
|---|---|---|---|---|---|
| | | | | **PREP** | **Obj.** |
| (a) The man was helpful. | | | I talked | *to* | *him*. |

|  |  | **Obj.** | **PREP** |  | |
|---|---|---|---|---|---|
| (b) The man | | *whom* | *I talked to* | | was helpful. |
| (c) The man | | *that* | *I talked to* | | was helpful. |
| (d) The man | | *Ø* | *I talked to* | | was helpful. |
| | **PREP** | **Obj.** | | | |
| (e) The man | *to* | *whom* | *I talked* | | was helpful. |

*Whom*, *which*, and *that* can be used as the object of a preposition in an adjective clause.

REMINDER: An object pronoun can be omitted from an adjective clause, as in (d) and (i).

In very formal English, a preposition comes at the beginning of an adjective clause, as in (e) and (j). The preposition is followed by either *whom* or *which* (not *that* or *who*), and the pronoun CANNOT be omitted.

| | | | | **PREP** | **Obj.** |
|---|---|---|---|---|---|
| (f) The chair is hard. | | | I am sitting | *in* | *it*. |

(b), (c), (d), and (e) have the same meaning.

| | **Obj.** | | **PREP** | |
|---|---|---|---|---|
| (g) The chair | *which* | *I am sitting in* | | is hard. |
| (h) The chair | *that* | *I am sitting in* | | is hard. |
| (i) The chair | *Ø* | *I am sitting in* | | is hard. |
| | **PREP** | **Obj.** | | |
| (j) The chair | *in* | *which* | *I am sitting* | is hard. |

(g), (h), (i), and (j) have the same meaning.

## 12-7　USING *WHOSE* IN ADJECTIVE CLAUSES

| | |
|---|---|
| (a) The man called the police. **His car** → **whose car** was stolen. | *Whose*★ shows possession. In (a): *His car* can be changed to *whose car* to make an adjective clause. In (b): *whose car was stolen* = an adjective clause. |
| (b) The man *whose car was stolen* called the police. | |
| (c) I know a girl. **Her brother** → **whose brother** is a movie star. | In (c): *Her brother* can be changed to *whose brother* to make an adjective clause. |
| (d) I know a girl *whose brother is a movie star*. | |
| (e) The people were friendly. We bought **their house.** → **whose house** | In (e): *Their house* can be changed to *whose house* to make an adjective clause. |
| (f) The people *whose house we bought* were friendly. | |

★*Whose* and *who's* have the same pronunciation but NOT the same meaning.
　*Who's* = *who is*: *Who's (Who is) your teacher?*

# CHAPTER 13
## Gerunds and Infinitives

## 13-1  VERB + GERUND

| | | |
|---|---|---|
| (a) I | verb    gerund<br>*enjoy*    *walking*    in the park. | A gerund is the *-ing* form of a verb. It is used as a noun. In (a): *walking* is a gerund. It is used as the object of the verb *enjoy*. |

| COMMON VERBS FOLLOWED BY GERUNDS | | | |
|---|---|---|---|
| *enjoy* | (b) | I *enjoy working* in my garden. | The verbs in the list are followed by gerunds. The list also contains phrasal verbs (e.g., *put off*) that are followed by gerunds. |
| *finish* | (c) | Ann *finished studying* at midnight. | |
| *stop* | (d) | It *stopped raining* a few minutes ago. | The verbs in the list are NOT followed by *to* + *the simple form of a verb* (an infinitive). |
| *quit* | (e) | David *quit smoking*. | |
| *mind* | (f) | Would you *mind opening* the window? | |
| *postpone* | (g) | I *postponed doing* my homework. | INCORRECT: *I enjoy to walk in the park.* |
| *put off* | (h) | I *put off doing* my homework. | INCORRECT: *Bob finished to study.* |
| *keep (on)* | (i) | *Keep (on) working.* Don't stop. | INCORRECT: *I'm thinking to go to Hawaii.* |
| *consider* | (j) | I*'m considering going* to Hawaii. | |
| *think about* | (k) | I*'m thinking about going* to Hawaii. | See Chart 2-5, p. 8, for the spelling of *-ing* verb forms. |
| *discuss* | (l) | They *discussed getting* a new car. | |
| *talk about* | (m) | They *talked about getting* a new car. | |

| | |
|---|---|
| (n) I *considered not going* to class. | Negative form: *not* + *gerund* |

## 13-2 GO + -ING

| | |
|---|---|
| (a) **Did** you **go shopping** yesterday?<br>(b) I **went swimming** last week.<br>(c) Bob **hasn't gone fishing** in years. | **Go** is followed by a gerund in certain idiomatic expressions about activities.<br>Notice: There is no **to** between **go** and the gerund.<br>INCORRECT: *Did you go to shopping?* |

**COMMON EXPRESSIONS WITH GO + -ING**

| | | | | |
|---|---|---|---|---|
| go boating | go dancing | go jogging | go (window) shopping | go (water) skiing |
| go bowling | go fishing | go running | go sightseeing | go skydiving |
| go camping | go hiking | go sailing | go (ice) skating | go swimming |

## 13-3 VERB + INFINITIVE

| | |
|---|---|
| (a) Tom **offered to lend** me some money.<br>(b) I've **decided to buy** a new car. | Some verbs are followed by an infinitive:<br>AN INFINITIVE = **to** + *the simple form of a verb.* |
| (c) I've **decided not to keep** my old car. | Negative form: **not** + *infinitive.* |

**COMMON VERBS FOLLOWED BY INFINITIVES**

| | | | | |
|---|---|---|---|---|
| want | hope | decide | seem | learn (how) |
| need | expect | promise | appear | try |
| would like | plan | offer | pretend | |
| would love | intend | agree | | (can't) afford |
| | mean | refuse | forget | (can't) wait |

## 13-4 VERB + GERUND OR INFINITIVE

| | |
|---|---|
| (a) It *began **raining***. <br> (b) It *began **to rain***. | Some verbs are followed by either a gerund or an infinitive. Usually there is no difference in meaning. (a) and (b) have the same meaning. |

**COMMON VERBS FOLLOWED BY EITHER A GERUND OR AN INFINITIVE**

| | | |
|---|---|---|
| *begin* | *like** | *hate* |
| *start* | *love** | *can't stand* |
| *continue* | | |

*COMPARE: ***Like*** and ***love*** can be followed by either a gerund or an infinitive:
  *I like going/to go to movies. I love playing/to play chess.*
**Would like** and **would love** are followed by infinitives:
  *I would like **to go** to a movie tonight. I'd love **to play** a game of chess right now.*

## 13-5 PREPOSITION + GERUND

| | |
|---|---|
| (a) Kate *insisted **on coming*** with us. <br> (b) We're *excited **about going*** to Tahiti. <br> (c) I *apologized **for being*** late. | A preposition is followed by a gerund, not an infinitive. In (a): The preposition *(on)* is followed by a gerund *(coming)*. |

**COMMON EXPRESSIONS WITH PREPOSITIONS FOLLOWED BY GERUNDS**

| | | |
|---|---|---|
| *be afraid **of*** (doing something) | *forgive* (someone) ***for*** | *plan **on*** |
| *apologize **for*** | *be good **at*** | *be responsible **for*** |
| *believe **in*** | *insist **on*** | *stop* (someone) ***from*** |
| *dream **about*** | *be interested **in*** | *thank* (someone) ***for*** |
| *be excited **about*** | *look forward **to*** | *be tired **of*** |
| *feel **like*** | *be nervous **about*** | *worry **about**/be worried **about*** |

Jake's not very *good*
***at cutting*** his own hair.

## 13-6  USING *BY* AND *WITH* TO EXPRESS HOW SOMETHING IS DONE

| | |
|---|---|
| (a) Pat turned off the tape recorder **by pushing** the stop button. | **By** + *a gerund* is used to express how something is done. |
| (b) Mary goes to work **by bus**.<br>(c) Andrea stirred her coffee **with a spoon**. | **By** or **with** followed by a noun is also used to express how something is done. |

**BY IS USED FOR MEANS OF TRANSPORTATION AND COMMUNICATION**

| | | | |
|---|---|---|---|
| *by (air)plane* ★ | *by subway* ★★ | *by mail* | *by air* |
| *by boat* | *by taxi* | *by (tele)phone* | *by land* |
| *by bus* | *by train* | *by fax* | *by sea* |
| *by car* | *by foot* (OR *on foot*) | *by e-mail* | |

**OTHERS**

| | | |
|---|---|---|
| *by chance* | *by mistake* | *by check* (but *in cash*) |
| *by choice* | *by hand* ★★★ | *by credit card* |

**WITH IS USED FOR INSTRUMENTS OR PARTS OF THE BODY**

I cut down the tree *with an ax* (by using an ax).
I swept the floor *with a broom*.
She pointed to a spot on the map *with her finger*.

★*airplane* = American English; *aeroplane* = British English.

★★*by subway* = American English; *by underground, by tube* = British English.

★★★The expression **by hand** is usually used to mean that something was made by a person, not by a machine: *This rug was made by hand*. (A person, not a machine, made this rug.)
   COMPARE: *I touched his shoulder **with my hand**.*

## 13-7  USING GERUNDS AS SUBJECTS; USING *IT* + INFINITIVE

| | |
|---|---|
| (a) **Riding** horses is fun.<br>(b) **It** is fun **to ride** horses.<br>(c) **Coming** to class on time is important.<br>(d) **It** is important **to come** to class on time. | (a) and (b) have the same meaning.<br>In (a): A gerund *(riding)* is the subject of the sentence.★  Notice: The verb *(is)* is singular because a gerund is singular.<br>In (b): The word *it* is used as the subject of the sentence.  The word *it* has the same meaning as the infinitive phrase at the end of the sentence: *it* means *to ride horses.* |

★It is also correct (but less common) to use an infinitive as the subject of a sentence: *To ride horses is fun.*

## 13-8 IT + INFINITIVE: USING FOR (SOMEONE)

| | |
|---|---|
| (a) *You* should study hard.<br>(b) It is important *for you* to study hard.<br><br>(c) *Mary* should study hard.<br>(d) It is important *for Mary* to study hard.<br><br>(e) *We* don't have to go to the meeting.<br>(f) It isn't necessary *for us* to go to the meeting.<br><br>(g) *A dog* can't talk.<br>(h) It is impossible *for a dog* to talk. | (a) and (b) have a similar meaning.<br>Notice the pattern in (b):<br><br>    *it is* + adjective + *for* (someone) + infinitive  phrase |

## 13-9 EXPRESSING PURPOSE WITH IN ORDER TO AND FOR

| | |
|---|---|
|    —*Why did you go to the post office?*<br>(a) I went to the post office *because I wanted to mail a letter.*<br>(b) I went to the post office *in order to mail* a letter.<br>(c) I went to the post office *to mail* a letter. | *In order to* expresses purpose.  It answers the question "Why?" |
| | In (c): *in order* is frequently omitted.<br>(a), (b), and (c) have the same meaning. |
| (d) I went to the post office *for* some stamps.<br>(e) I went to the post office *to buy* some stamps.<br>  INCORRECT: *I went to the post office for to buy some stamps.*<br>  INCORRECT: *I went to the post office for buying some stamps.* | *For* is also used to express purpose, but it is a preposition and is followed by a noun phrase, as in (d). |

## 13-10 USING INFINITIVES WITH TOO AND ENOUGH

| | |
|---|---|
| **TOO** + **ADJECTIVE** + **(FOR SOMEONE)** + **INFINITIVE**<br>(a) A piano is   *too heavy*              *to lift.*<br>(b) That box is  *too heavy*  *for me*     *to lift.*<br>(c) That box is  *too heavy*  *for Bob*    *to lift.* | Infinitives often follow expressions with *too*.<br>*Too* comes in front of an adjective.<br>In the speaker's mind, the use of *too* implies a negative result.<br>COMPARE<br>*The box is too heavy. I can't lift it.*<br>*The box is very heavy, but I can lift it.* |
| **ENOUGH** + **NOUN** + **INFINITIVE**<br>(d) I don't have   **enough** *money*   **to** *buy* that car.<br>(e) Did you have   **enough** *time*   **to** *finish* the test? | |
| **ADJECTIVE** + **ENOUGH** + **INFINITIVE**<br>(f) Jimmy isn't        *old* **enough**    **to** *go* to school.<br>(g) Are you        *hungry* **enough**   **to** *eat* three sandwiches? | Infinitives often follow expressions with **enough**.<br>**Enough** comes in front of a noun.★<br>**Enough** follows an adjective. |

★**Enough** can also follow a noun: *I don't have* **money enough** *to buy that car.*  In everyday English, however, **enough** usually comes in front of a noun.

# CHAPTER 14
## Noun Clauses

## CONTENTS

## 14-1  NOUN CLAUSES: INTRODUCTION

| | |
|---|---|
| **S  V         O**<br>(a) I know  \|**his address**\|.<br>    (noun phrase) | Verbs are often followed by objects. The object is usually a noun phrase.★<br>In (a): **his address** is a noun phrase;<br>   **his address** is the object of the verb *know*. |
| **S  V         O**<br>(b) I know  \|**where he lives**\|.<br>    (noun clause) | Some verbs can be followed by noun clauses.★<br>In (b): **where he lives** is a noun clause;<br>   **where he lives** is the object of the verb *know*. |
| **         O**<br>**S  V  ┌   S   V   ┐**<br>(c) I know  *where he lives*. | A noun clause has its own subject and verb.<br>In (c): *he* is the subject of the noun clause; *lives* is the verb of the noun clause. |
| (d) I know **where my book is**.<br>        (noun clause) | A noun clause can begin with a question word.<br>(See Chart 14-2, p. 90.) |
| (e) I don't know **if Ed is married**.<br>        (noun clause) | A noun clause can begin with *if* or *whether*.<br>(See Chart 14-4, p. 91.) |
| (f) I know **that the world is round**.<br>        (noun clause) | A noun clause can begin with *that*. (See Chart 14-5, p. 91.) |

★A **phrase** is a group of related words. It does not contain a subject and a verb.
  A **clause** is a group of related words. It contains a subject and a verb.

## 14-2  NOUN CLAUSES THAT BEGIN WITH A QUESTION WORD

These question words can be used to introduce a noun clause: *when, where, why, how, who, whom, what, which, whose*.

| INFORMATION QUESTION | NOUN CLAUSE | Notice in the examples: Usual question word order is NOT used in a noun clause. |
|---|---|---|
| (a) Where *does he live?*<br>(c) When *did they leave?*<br>(e) What *did she say?*<br>(g) Why *is Tom* absent? | (b) I don't know *where he lives.*<br>(d) Do you know *when they left?*\*<br>(f) Please tell me *what she said.*<br>(h) I wonder *why Tom is* absent. | INCORRECT: *I know where does he live.*<br>CORRECT: *I know where he lives.* |
| (i) *Who came* to class?<br>(k) *What happened?* | (j) I don't know *who came to class.*<br>(l) Tell me *what happened.* | In (i) and (j): Question word order and noun clause word order are the same when the question word is used as a subject. |

\*A question mark is used at the end of this noun clause because the main subject and the verb of the sentence *(Do you know)* are in question word order.

Example: *Do you know when they left?*

*Do you know* asks a question; *when they left* is a noun clause.

Do you know *when the first wheel **was** invented?*

## 14-3  NOUN CLAUSES WITH *WHO, WHAT, WHOSE + BE*

| QUESTION | NOUN CLAUSE | |
|---|---|---|
| (a) Who **is** *that boy*?<br>    V   S<br>(c) Whose pen **is** *this*?<br>        V  S | (b) Tell me *who **that boy** is.*<br>        S   V<br>(d) Tell me *whose pen **this** is.*<br>           S  V | A noun or pronoun that follows main verb **be** in a question comes in front of **be** in a noun clause, as in (b) and (d). |
| (e) **Who** **is** in the office?<br>   S   V<br>(g) **Whose pen** **is** on the desk?<br>    S      V | (f) Tell me **who** **is** *in the office.*<br>       S   V<br>(h) Tell me **whose pen** **is** *on the desk.*<br>        S     V | A prepositional phrase (e.g., *in the office*) does not come in front of **be** in a noun clause, as in (f) and (h). |

## 14-4 NOUN CLAUSES THAT BEGIN WITH *IF* OR *WHETHER*

| YES/NO QUESTION | NOUN CLAUSE | |
|---|---|---|
| (a) Is Eric at home?<br>(c) Does the bus stop here?<br>(e) Did Alice go to Chicago? | (b) I don't know *if Eric is at home*.<br>(d) Do you know *if the bus stops here?*<br>(f) I wonder *if Alice went to Chicago*. | When a yes/no question is changed to a noun clause, *if* is usually used to introduce the clause.★ |

| | |
|---|---|
| (g) I don't know *if Eric is at home **or not***. | When *if* introduces a noun clause, the expression *or not* sometimes comes at the end of the clause, as in (g). |
| (h) I don't know ***whether** Eric is at home (or not)*. | In (h): ***whether*** has the same meaning as *if*. |

★See Chart 14-11, p. 95, for the use of *if* with *ask* in reported speech.

Susie wants to know *if there is a pot of gold at the end of the rainbow.*

## 14-5 NOUN CLAUSES THAT BEGIN WITH *THAT*

| | |
|---|---|
|    S    V            O<br>(a) I think *that Mr. Jones is a good teacher.*<br>(b) I hope ***that*** *you can come to the game.*<br>(c) Mary realizes ***that*** *she should study harder.*<br>(d) I dreamed ***that*** *I was on the top of a mountain.* | A noun clause can be introduced by the word ***that***.<br>In (a): *that Mr. Jones is a good teacher* is a noun clause. It is the object of the verb *think*.<br>*That*-clauses are frequently used as the objects of verbs that express mental activity. (See the list below.) |
| (e) *I think **that** Mr. Jones is a good teacher.*<br>(f) *I think Ø Mr. Jones is a good teacher.* | The word ***that*** is often omitted, especially in speaking. (e) and (f) have the same meaning. |

**COMMON VERBS FOLLOWED BY *THAT*-CLAUSES★**

| | | | |
|---|---|---|---|
| *assume that* | *feel that* | *learn that* | *read that* |
| *believe that* | *hear that* | *notice that* | *say that* |
| *discover that* | *hope that* | *predict that* | *suppose that* |
| *dream that* | *know that* | *prove that* | *think that* |

★The verbs in the above list are those that are emphasized in the exercises. Some other common verbs that can be followed by *that*-clauses are:

| | | | | |
|---|---|---|---|---|
| *agree that* | *fear that* | *imagine that* | *realize that* | *reveal that* |
| *conclude that* | *figure out that* | *indicate that* | *recall that* | *show that* |
| *decide that* | *find out that* | *observe that* | *recognize that* | *suspect that* |
| *demonstrate that* | *forget that* | *presume that* | *regret that* | *teach that* |
| *doubt that* | *guess that* | *pretend that* | *remember that* | *understand that* |

## 14-6  OTHER USES OF *THAT*-CLAUSES

| | |
|---|---|
| (a) I'm **sure that** the bus stops here. <br> (b) I'm **glad that** you're feeling better today. <br> (c) I'm **sorry that** I missed class yesterday. <br> (d) I **was disappointed that** the peace conference failed. | *That*-clauses can follow certain expressions with **be** + *adjective* or **be** + *past participle*. <br> The word **that** can be omitted with no change in meaning: <br>     *I'm sure Ø the bus stops here.* |
| (e) **It is true that** the world is round. <br> (f) **It is a fact that** the world is round. | Two common expressions followed by *that*-clauses are: <br>     *It is true (that) ....* <br>     *It is a fact (that) ....* |

**COMMON EXPRESSIONS FOLLOWED BY *THAT*-CLAUSES★**

| | | | |
|---|---|---|---|
| *be afraid that* | *be disappointed that* | *be sorry that* | *It is true that* |
| *be aware that* | *be glad that* | *be sure that* | *It is a fact that* |
| *be certain that* | *be happy that* | *be surprised that* | |
| *be convinced that* | *be pleased that* | *be worried that* | |

★The above list contains expressions emphasized in the exercises. Some other common expressions with **be** that are frequently followed by *that*-clauses are:

| | | | |
|---|---|---|---|
| *be amazed that* | *be delighted that* | *be impressed that* | *be sad that* |
| *be angry that* | *be fortunate that* | *be lucky that* | *be shocked that* |
| *be ashamed that* | *be furious that* | *be positive that* | *be terrified that* |
| *be astounded that* | *be horrified that* | *be proud that* | *be thrilled that* |

## 14-7  SUBSTITUTING *SO* FOR A *THAT*-CLAUSE IN CONVERSATIONAL RESPONSES

| | |
|---|---|
| (a) A: Is Ana from Peru? <br>     B: **I think so.** *(so = that Ana is from Peru)* <br> (b) A: Does Judy live in Dallas? <br>     B: **I believe so.** *(so = that Judy lives in Dallas)* <br> (c) A: Did you pass the test? <br>     B: **I hope so.** *(so = that I passed the test)* | **Think**, **believe**, and **hope** are frequently followed by **so** in conversational English in response to a yes/no question. They are alternatives to *yes, no,* or *I don't know.* <br> **So** replaces a *that*-clause. <br> *INCORRECT: I think so that Ana is from Peru.* |
| (d) A: Is Jack married? <br>     B: **I don't think so.** / **I don't believe so.** | Negative usage of **think so** and **believe so**: <br>     *do not think so / do not believe so* |
| (e) A: Did you fail the test? <br>     B: **I hope *not*.** | Negative usage of **hope** in conversational responses: <br> *hope not.* <br> In (e): *I hope not = I hope I didn't fail the test.* <br> *INCORRECT: I don't hope so.* |
| (f) A: Do you want to come with us? <br>     B: Oh, I don't know. **I guess *so*.** | Other common conversational responses: <br>     *I guess so. I guess not.* <br>     *I suppose so. I suppose not.* |

## 14-8 QUOTED SPEECH

Sometimes we want to quote a speaker's words—to write a speaker's exact words. Exact quotations are used in many kinds of writing, such as newspaper articles, stories and novels, and academic papers. When we quote a speaker's words, we use quotation marks.

| | |
|---|---|
| (a) **SPEAKERS' EXACT WORDS**<br>Jane: Cats are fun to watch.<br>Mike: Yes, I agree. They're graceful and playful. Do you own a cat? | (b) **QUOTING THE SPEAKERS' WORDS**<br>Jane said, **"**Cats are fun to watch**."**<br>Mike said, **"Y**es, I agree. They're graceful and playful. Do you own a cat**?"** |

(c) **HOW TO WRITE QUOTATIONS**
1. Add a comma after *said*.★ ⟶ Jane said,
2. Add quotation marks.★★ ⟶ Jane said, "
3. Capitalize the first word of the quotation. ⟶ Jane said, "Cats
4. Write the quotation. Add a final period. ⟶ Jane said, "Cats are fun to watch.
5. Add quotation marks **after** the period. ⟶ Jane said, "Cats are fun to watch."

| | |
|---|---|
| (d) Mike said, "Yes, I agree. They're graceful and playful. Do you own a cat?"<br><br>(e) *INCORRECT: Mike said, "Yes, I agree." "They're graceful and playful." "Do you own a cat?"* | When there are two (or more) sentences in a quotation, put the quotation marks at the beginning and end of the whole quote, as in (d). Do not put quotation marks around each sentence. As with a period, put the quotation marks after a question mark at the end of a quote. |

| | |
|---|---|
| (f) "Cats are fun to watch," Jane said.<br><br>(g) "Do you own a cat?" Mike asked. | In (f): Notice that a comma (not a period) is used at the end of the quoted **sentence** when *Jane said* comes after the quote.<br><br>In (g): Notice that a question mark (not a comma) is used at the end of the quoted **question**. |

*Other common verbs besides *say* that introduce questions: *admit, announce, answer, ask, complain, explain, inquire, report, reply, shout, state, write*.

**Quotation marks are called "inverted commas" in British English.

The fox said, "I'm going to eat you."
The rabbit said, "You have to catch me first!"

## 14-9 QUOTED SPEECH vs. REPORTED SPEECH

| QUOTED SPEECH<br>(a) Ann said, "*I'm* hungry."<br>(b) Tom said, "*I need* my pen." | **Quoted speech** = giving a speaker's exact words. Quotation marks are used.★ |
|---|---|
| REPORTED SPEECH<br>(c) Ann said (that) *she was* hungry.<br>(d) Tom said (that) *he needed* his pen. | **Reported speech** = giving the idea of a speaker's words. Not all of the exact words are used; pronouns and verb forms may change. Quotation marks are NOT used.★ |

★*Quoted speech* is also called "direct speech." *Reported speech* is also called "indirect speech."

## 14-10   VERB FORMS IN REPORTED SPEECH

| (a) QUOTED: Joe said, "I *feel* good."<br>(b) REPORTED: Joe said he *felt* good.<br>(c) QUOTED: Sue said, "I *am* happy."<br>(d) REPORTED: Sue said she *was* happy. | In formal English, if the reporting verb (e.g., *said*) is in the past, the verb in the noun clause is often also in a past form, as in (b) and (d). |
|---|---|
| —Ann said, "I am hungry."<br>(e) A: What did Ann just say?  I didn't hear her.<br>   B: She said she *is* hungry.<br>(f) A: What did Ann say when she got home last night?<br>   B: She said she *was* hungry. | In informal English, often the verb in the noun clause is not changed to a past form, especially when words are reported *soon after* they are said, as in (e).<br><br>In *later reporting*, however, or in formal English, a past verb is commonly used, as in (f). |
| (g) Ann *says* (that) she *is* hungry. | If the reporting verb is present tense (e.g., *says)*, no change is made in the noun clause verb. |

| QUOTED SPEECH | REPORTED SPEECH<br>*formal or later reporting* | REPORTED SPEECH<br>*informal or immediate reporting* |
|---|---|---|
| He said, "I *work* hard." | He said he *worked* hard. | He said he *works* hard. |
| He said, "I *am working* hard." | He said he *was working* hard. | He said he *is working* hard. |
| He said, "I *worked* hard." | He said he *had worked* hard. | He said he *worked* hard. |
| He said, "I *have worked* hard." | He said he *had worked* hard. | He said he *has worked* hard. |
| He said, "I *am going to work* hard." | He said he *was going to work* hard. | He said he *is going to work* hard. |
| He said, "I *will work* hard." | He said he *would work* hard. | He said he *will work* hard. |
| He said, "I *can work* hard." | He said he *could work* hard. | He said he *can work* hard. |

## 14-11 COMMON REPORTING VERBS: *TELL, ASK, ANSWER/REPLY*

| | |
|---|---|
| (a) Ann **said** that she was hungry. <br> (b) Ann **told me** that she was hungry. <br> (c) Ann **told Tom** that she was hungry. <br>     INCORRECT: *Ann told that she was hungry* <br>     INCORRECT: *Ann said me that she was hungry.* | A main verb that introduces reported speech is called a "reporting verb." **Say** is the most common reporting verb★ and is usually followed immediately by a noun clause, as in (a). <br> **Tell** is also commonly used. Note that **told** is followed by **me** in (b) and by **Tom** in (c). <br> **Tell** needs to be followed immediately by a (pro)noun object and then by a noun clause. |
| (d) QUOTED: Sue said (to me), "Are you tired?" <br>     REPORTED: Sue **asked** *(me)* **if** I was tired. <br> (e) Sue **wanted to know if** I was tired. <br>     Sue **wondered if** I was tired. <br>     Sue **inquired whether or not** I was tired. | **Asked**, not **said**, is used to report questions. <br><br> Questions are also reported by using **want to know, wonder,** and **inquire**. |
| (f) QUOTED: I said (to Ann), "I am not tired." <br>     REPORTED: I **answered**/**replied** that I wasn't tired. | The verbs **answer** and **reply** are often used to report replies. |

★Other common reporting verbs: *Ann **announced, commented, complained, explained, remarked, stated** that she was hungry.*

Mrs. Ball **asked** her husband *if* he could help her
clean the closet. Her husband **replied** that he was busy.
He **told** *her that* he was fixing his zipper.

# APPENDIX *1*
## Phrasal Verbs

## CONTENTS

## A1-1  PHRASAL VERBS: INTRODUCTION

| | |
|---|---|
| (a) We **put off** our trip.  We'll go next month instead of this month.  *(put off = postpone)* | In (a): *put off* = a phrasal verb. |
| (b) Jimmy, **put on** your coat before you go outdoors. *(put on = place clothes on one's body)* | A phrasal verb = a verb and a particle that together have a special meaning.  For example, *put off* means "postpone." |
| (c) Someone left the scissors on the table.  They didn't belong there.  I **put** them **away**.  *(put away = put something in its usual or proper place)* | A particle = a "small word" (e.g., *off, on, away back*) that is used in a phrasal verb. |
| (d) After I used the dictionary, I **put** it **back** on the shelf.  *(put back = return something to its original place)* | Note that the phrasal verbs with *put* in (a), (b), (c), and (d) all have different meanings. |

| **SEPARABLE** | Some phrasal verbs are **separable**: a NOUN |
|---|---|
| (e) We *put **off** our **trip***. = (vb + **particle** + NOUN) | OBJECT can either |
| (f) We *put our **trip** off*. = (vb + NOUN + **particle**) | (1)  follow the particle, as in (e), OR (2)  come between (separate) the verb and the particle, as in (f). |
| (g) We *put **it** off*.       = (vb + PRONOUN + **particle**) | If a phrasal verb is separable, a PRONOUN OBJECT comes between the verb and the particle, as in (g). *INCORRECT: We put off it.* |

| **NONSEPARABLE** | If a phrasal verb is **nonseparable**, a NOUN or |
|---|---|
| (h) I *ran **into** Bob*.       = (vb + **particle** + NOUN) | PRONOUN always follows (never precedes) the particle, as in (h) and (i). |
| (i) I *ran **into** him*.       = (vb + **particle** + PRONOUN) | *INCORRECT: I ran Bob into.* *INCORRECT: I ran him into.* |

## A1-2 PHRASAL VERBS: INTRANSITIVE

| | |
|---|---|
| (a) The machine *broke down*.<br>(b) Please *come in*.<br>(c) I *fell down*. | Some phrasal verbs are intransitive; i.e., they are not followed by an object. |

## A1-3 THREE-WORD PHRASAL VERBS

| | |
|---|---|
| | Some two-word verbs (e.g., **drop in**) can become three-word verbs (e.g., **drop in on**). |
| (a) Last night some friends **dropped in**. | In (a): **drop in** is not followed by an object. It is an intransitive phrasal verb (i.e., it is not followed by an object). |
| (b) Let's **drop in on** Alice this afternoon. | In (b): **drop in on** is a three-word phrasal verb. Three-word phrasal verbs are transitive (they are followed by objects). |
| (c) We *dropped in on* **her** last week. | In (c): Three-word phrasal verbs are nonseparable (the noun or pronoun follows the phrasal verb). |

"I have to go. I'll call you after I
***get through with*** dinner."

**A**  **ask out** . . . . . . . . . . . . . . . . . . . . . *ask (someone) to go on a date*

**B**  **blow out** . . . . . . . . . . . . . . . . . . . . . *extinguish (a match, a candle)*

    **break down** . . . . . . . . . . . . . . . . . . . *stop functioning properly*

    **break out** . . . . . . . . . . . . . . . . . . . . . *happen suddenly*

    **break up** . . . . . . . . . . . . . . . . . . . . . . *separate, end a relationship*

    **bring back** . . . . . . . . . . . . . . . . . . . . . *return*

    **bring up** . . . . . . . . . . . . . . . . . . . . . . *(1) raise (children)*

                                       *(2) mention, start to talk about*

**C**  **call back** . . . . . . . . . . . . . . . . . . . . . *return a telephone call*

    **call off** . . . . . . . . . . . . . . . . . . . . . . . *cancel*

    **call on** . . . . . . . . . . . . . . . . . . . . . . . *ask (someone) to speak in class*

    **call up** . . . . . . . . . . . . . . . . . . . . . . . *make a telephone call*

    **cheer up** . . . . . . . . . . . . . . . . . . . . . . *make happier*

    **clean up** . . . . . . . . . . . . . . . . . . . . . . *make neat and clean*

    **come along** (**with**) . . . . . . . . . . . . . . *accompany*

    **come from** . . . . . . . . . . . . . . . . . . . . . *originate*

    **come in** . . . . . . . . . . . . . . . . . . . . . . . *enter a room or building*

    **come over** (**to**) . . . . . . . . . . . . . . . . *visit the speaker's place*

    **cross out** . . . . . . . . . . . . . . . . . . . . . . *draw a line through*

    **cut out** (**of**) . . . . . . . . . . . . . . . . . . . *remove with scissors or knife*

**D**  **dress up** . . . . . . . . . . . . . . . . . . . . . . *put on nice clothes*

    **drop in** (**on**) . . . . . . . . . . . . . . . . . . *visit without calling first or without an invitation*

    **drop out** (**of**) . . . . . . . . . . . . . . . . . *stop attending (school)*

**E**  **eat out** . . . . . . . . . . . . . . . . . . . . . . . *eat outside of one's home*

**F**  **fall down** . . . . . . . . . . . . . . . . . . . . . *fall to the ground*

    **figure out** . . . . . . . . . . . . . . . . . . . . . *find the solution to a problem*

    **fill in** . . . . . . . . . . . . . . . . . . . . . . . . *complete by writing in a blank space*

    **fill out** . . . . . . . . . . . . . . . . . . . . . . . *write information on a form*

    **fill up** . . . . . . . . . . . . . . . . . . . . . . . . *fill completely with gas, water, coffee, etc.*

    **find out** (**about**) . . . . . . . . . . . . . . . . *discover information*

    **fool around** (**with**) . . . . . . . . . . . . . . *have fun while wasting time*

**G**  **get along** (**with**) . . . . . . . . . . . . . . . *have a good relationship with*

    **get back** (**from**) . . . . . . . . . . . . . . . . *return from (a trip)*

    **get in** . . . . . . . . . . . . . . . . . . . . . . . . *enter a car, a taxi*

    **get off** . . . . . . . . . . . . . . . . . . . . . . . *leave a bus/an airplane/a train/a subway*

    **get on** . . . . . . . . . . . . . . . . . . . . . . . *enter a bus/an airplane/a train/a subway*

    **get out of** . . . . . . . . . . . . . . . . . . . . . *leave a car, a taxi*

*For more information about phrasal verbs and their meanings, see dictionaries written especially for second language learners, such as the *Longman Advanced American Dictionary,* the *Longman Dictionary of Contemporary English,* the *Collins COBUILD English Learner's Dictionary,* or the *Oxford Advanced Learner's Dictionary.*

| | | |
|---|---|---|
| | **get over** | *recover from an illness or a shock* |
| | **get together** (**with**) | *join, meet* |
| | **get through** (**with**) | *finish* |
| | **get up** | *get out of bed in the morning* |
| | **give away** | *donate, get rid of by giving* |
| | **give back** | *return (something) to (someone)* |
| | **give up** | *quit doing (something) or quit trying* |
| | **go on** | *continue* |
| | **go back** (**to**) | *return to a place* |
| | **go out** | *not stay home* |
| | **go over** (**to**) | *(1) approach* |
| | | *(2) visit another's home* |
| | **grow up** (**in**) | *become an adult* |
| **H** | **hand in** | *give homework, test papers, etc., to a teacher* |
| | **hand out** | *give (something) to this person, then to that person, then to another person, etc.* |
| | **hang around/out** (**with**) | *spend undirected time* |
| | **hang up** | *(1) hang on a hanger or a hook* |
| | | *(2) end a telephone conversation* |
| | **have on** | *wear* |
| | **help out** | *assist (someone)* |
| **K** | **keep away** (**from**) | *not give to* |
| | **keep on** | *continue* |
| **L** | **lay off** | *stop employment* |
| | **leave on** | *(1) not turn off (a light, a machine)* |
| | | *(2) not take off (clothing)* |
| | **look into** | *investigate* |
| | **look over** | *examine carefully* |
| | **look out** (**for**) | *be careful* |
| | **look up** | *look for information in a dictionary, a telephone directory,n an encyclopedia, etc.* |
| **M** | **make up** | *invent (a story)* |
| | **move in** (**to**) | *start living in a new home* |
| | **move out** (**of**) | *stop living at a place* |
| **P** | **pay back** | *return borrowed money to (someone)* |
| | **pick up** | *lift* |
| | **point out** | *call attention to* |
| | **print out** | *create a paper copy from a computer* |
| | **put away** | *put (something) in its usual or proper place* |
| | **put back** | *return (something) to its original place* |

|  |  |  |
|---|---|---|
|  | **put down** | *stop holding or carrying* |
|  | **put off** | *postpone* |
|  | **put on** | *put clothes on one's body* |
|  | **put out** | *extinguish (stop) a fire, a cigarette* |
| **R** | **run into** | *meet by chance* |
|  | **run out (of)** | *finish the supply of (something)* |
| **S** | **set out (for)** | *begin a trip* |
|  | **shut off** | *stop a machine or a light, turn off* |
|  | **sign up (for)** | *put one's name on a list* |
|  | **show up** | *come, appear* |
|  | **sit around (with)** | *sit and do nothing* |
|  | **sit back** | *put one's back against a chair back* |
|  | **sit down** | *go from standing to sitting* |
|  | **speak up** | *speak louder* |
|  | **stand up** | *go from sitting to standing* |
|  | **start over** | *begin again* |
|  | **stay up** | *not go to bed* |
| **T** | **take back** | *return* |
|  | **take off** | *(1) remove clothes from one's body* |
|  |  | *(2) ascend in an airplane* |
|  | **take out** | *invite out and pay* |
|  | **talk over** | *discuss* |
|  | **tear down** | *destroy a building* |
|  | **tear out (of)** | *remove (paper) by tearing* |
|  | **tear up** | *tear into small pieces* |
|  | **think over** | *consider* |
|  | **throw away/out** | *put in the trash, discard* |
|  | **try on** | *put on clothing to see if it fits* |
|  | **turn around** } **turn back** } | *change to the opposite direction* |
|  | **turn down** | *decrease the volume* |
|  | **turn off** | *stop a machine or a light* |
|  | **turn on** | *start a machine or a light* |
|  | **turn over** | *turn the top side to the bottom* |
|  | **turn up** | *increase the volume* |
| **W** | **wake up** | *stop sleeping* |
|  | **watch out (for)** | *be careful* |
|  | **work out** | *solve* |
|  | **write down** | *write a note on a piece of paper* |

# *APPENDIX* **2**
## Preposition Combinations

## A2-1   PREPOSITION COMBINATIONS: INTRODUCTION

|  |  |
|---|---|
|       adj   + prep<br>(a)  Ali is ***absent   from***   class today.<br><br>      verb  + prep<br>(b)  This book ***belongs   to***   me. | *At, from, of, on,* and *to* are examples of prepositions.*<br><br>Prepositions are often combined with adjectives, as in (a), and verbs, as in (b). |

*See Chart A2-2 for a list of prepositions.

Jack's thermos bottle is ***full of*** coffee.

# A2-2 PREPOSITION COMBINATIONS: A REFERENCE LIST

**A**
*be* absent from
*be* accustomed to
  add *(this)* to *(that)*
*be* acquainted with
  admire *(someone)* for *(something)*
*be* afraid of
  agree with *(someone)* about *(something)*
*be* angry at / with *(someone)* about / over *(something)*
  apologize to *(someone)* for *(something)*
  apply for *(something)*
  approve of
  argue with *(someone)* about / over *(something)*
    arrive at *(a building / a room)*
    arrive in *(a city / a country)*
  ask *(someone)* about *(something)*
  ask *(someone)* for *(something)*
*be* aware of

**B**
*be* bad for
  believe in
  belong to
*be* bored with / by
  borrow *(something)* from *(someone)*

**C**
*be* clear to
  combine with
  compare *(this)* to / with *(that)*
  complain to *(someone)* about *(something)*
*be* composed of
  concentrate on
  consist of
*be* crazy about
*be* crowded with
*be* curious about

**D**
  depend on *(someone)* for *(something)*
*be* dependent on *(someone)* for *(something)*
*be* devoted to
  die of / from
*be* different from
  disagree with *(someone)* about *(something)*
*be* disappointed in
  discuss *(something)* with *(someone)*
  divide *(this)* into *(that)*
*be* divorced from

*be* done with
  dream about / of
  dream of

**E**
*be* engaged to
*be* equal to
  escape from *(a place)*
*be* excited about
  excuse *(someone)* for *(something)*
  excuse from
*be* exhausted from

**F**
*be* familiar with
*be* famous for
  feel about
  feel like
  fill *(something)* with
*be* finished with
  forgive *(someone)* for *(something)*
*be* friendly to / with
*be* frightened of / by
*be* full of

**G**
  get rid of
*be* gone from
*be* good for
  graduate from

**H**
  happen to
*be* happy about *(something)*
*be* happy for *(someone)*
  hear about / of *(something)* from *(someone)*
  help *(someone)* with *(something)*
  hide *(something)* from *(someone)*
  hope for
*be* hungry for

**I**
  insist on
*be* interested in
  introduce *(someone)* to *(someone)*
  invite *(someone)* to *(something)*
*be* involved in

**K**
*be* kind to
  know about

**L**

laugh at
leave for *(a place)*
listen to
look at
look for
look forward to
look like

**M**

*be* made of
*be* married to
matter to
*be* the matter with
multiply *(this)* by *(that)*

**N**

*be* nervous about
*be* nice to

**O**

*be* opposed to

**P**

pay for
*be* patient with
*be* pleased with / about
play with
point at
*be* polite to
prefer *(this)* to *(that)*
*be* prepared for
protect *(this)* from *(that)*
provide *(someone)* with
*be* proud of

**Q**

*be* qualified for

**R**

read about
*be* ready for

*be* related to
rely on
*be* responsible for

**S**

*be* sad about
*be* satisfied with
*be* scared of / by
search for
separate *(this)* from *(that)*
*be* similar to
speak to / with *(someone)* about *(something)*
stare at
subtract *(this)* from *(that)*
*be* sure of / about

**T**

take care of
talk about *(something)*
talk to / with *(someone)* about *(something)*
tell *(someone)* about *(something)*
*be* terrified of / by
thank *(someone)* for *(something)*
think about / of
*be* thirsty for
*be* tired from
*be* tired of
translate from *(one language)* to *(another)*

**U**

*be* used to

**W**

wait for
wait on
warn about / of
wonder about
*be* worried about

# INDEX

| | |
|---|---|
| **After,** 12, 17, 40<br>    *(Look on pages 12, 17, and 40.)* | The numbers following the words listed in the index refer to page numbers in the text. |
| Consonants, 4*fn.*<br>    *(Look at the footnote on page 4.)* | Information given in the footnotes to charts and exercises is noted by the page number plus the abbreviation *fn.* |

# NOTES

# NOTES

# NOTES

# NOTES